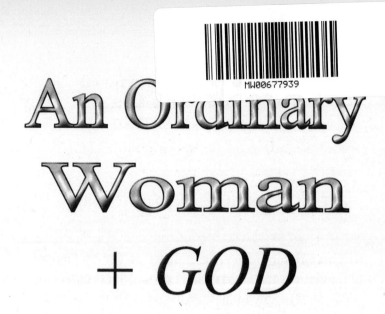

An Ordinary Woman

+ *GOD*

by

Dorothy Hunt

McDougal Publishing is a ministry of The McDougal
Foundation, Inc., a Maryland nonprofit corporation
dedicated to spreading the Gospel of the Lord Jesus
Christ to as many people as possible
in the shortest time possible.

Published by:

McDougal Publishing
P.O. Box 3595
Hagerstown, MD 21742-3595

www.mcdougalpublishing.com

ISBN: 978-1-58158-181-2

Printed in the United States of America
For Worldwide Distribution

DEDICATION

This book is dedicated to all the people who inspired me to write and share my story with others who will read how God can take an uneducated woman and show her that nothing is impossible with Him. To God be all the glory.

To Phyliss & Omar
from Pastor Dorothy
Hunt
2-14-14

CONTENTS

CHAPTER 1

THE BEGINNING

IN 1927, AT NORTH Hudson in Wee Hawken, New Jersey, I was born. My mother was a Virginia belle, born in Richmond, and my dad was an immigrant from Italy, who came to this country at four years of age. He was stationed in the Army at Fort Lee, Virginia, when he met Mother and swept her off her feet, and they got married.

My mom and dad, the Logios, were always in business. Dad knew how to make money in whatever he did. They had a store, and my sister Margaret and I were always in the store with them from an early age. The candy case had a lock on it so that we couldn't get into it. One day I had the bright idea of taking a broom and pushing the lock off. It worked. You probably know what happened next. We ate a lot of candy and got caught, and Dad taught us a hard lesson that day.

When I was five, Dad met some people named O'Larry. They were circus people who had money, and they owned land in Henderson, North Carolina. One day Mr. O'Larry asked Dad if he would be interested in moving to Henderson and running a new diner there for them. That is how our family came to live in Henderson.

The diner was located on a railroad car. It was brand new, and looked like a silver bullet, inside and out. The day it arrived in Henderson by train the whole town came out to see it and meet the new folks who had come to town to operate it. Dad, being a very friendly person, invited everyone in town to come and try some of his cooking. The first meal would be free. Soon he had a booming business.

Dad would bake fresh pies every day, and he quickly learned that the people of Henderson liked navy beans and corn bread, and so he made what they liked. They also came to like some of his famous Italian dishes.

We were all very happy: Dad, cooked and sang, Mom, worked as one of the waitresses and as cashier, and when we came home from school, my sister and I helped clean the tables. Soon Dad had enough friends that he started a girls' softball team and then a men's team.

God was never mentioned in our family, unless it was a curse word. We were all too busy making money to go to church.

In the summer, when school was out for the season, Mom would put me on the bus to go spend the summer with her two sisters, Aunt Ethel (who never married) and Aunt Millie, and also our beloved Grandpa.

Grandpa was already in his eighties, but he would get up and dress and go stand by the bank on the corner to flirt with girls as they went to work.

The first remembrance I have of church was when Aunt Ethel sent me to a church nearby one day. All I remember about that visit is that I sat in a pretty white chair with a bow on it, and the people sang *Happy Birthday* to me. Even then, God had his hand on me and had chosen me, but I didn't know it yet.

My aunts took me to Miller & Rhodes downtown and bought me pretty dresses.

I was also put on a train to go spend time with Dad's parents, Grandpa and Grandma Logio. They loved me and were very good to me.

My grandmother Logio was a holy woman. Every morning at 7:00 A.M. she would go to Mass and pray. Sometimes she let me go with her, but I didn't understand what it was all about. Every night, Grandpa would sit at the table and read his Bible.

Grandpa was a blacksmith and shoed horses, but they raised ten children and sent nine of them to college. Grandma stayed home and looked after the children. Their youngest daughter, Careen, was two years younger than I. She was my aunt, but we were also best friends.

Grandma made her own spaghetti and pretzels. She knew I loved her spaghetti, so she would say, "Put on the sauce; Dorothy is here." She was not a big person, but you'd better not disobey her. One day her son, Vinnie, who was home from the Army, sassed her, and she picked up a broom and chased him all over the house.

Eventually he jumped behind the couch, but she got him anyway.

There was no television in those days, so we would sit in front of the radio in the evenings or sing. My favorite song that Grandma sang was *O, Solo Mio*. I still love that song. It is sung to God, when it says. "Oh, how I love You!"

We would sometimes sit out on the front porch, and Grandpa would give us a penny for every fly we killed. He also taught me how to say "Close the door" in Italian. He would ask me, in Italian, "Where is your mouth?" or eyes, nose, and ears, and then he would laugh. He would put me on his knee and sing *It's Three O'clock in the Morning*. What wonderful memories I have of those happy days!

As time went on, our lives changed.

CHAPTER 2

UPHEAVAL

WHEN I WAS FOURTEEN and Margie was twelve, Dad left us and ran off with one of the waitresses to New York. Now Mom had to work very long hours to support us. Margie and I went straight to the diner after school and worked until about 6:00 and then went on home to do our homework and get ready for school the next day. Mom came home much later, so we were left unsupervised.

By the time I was fifteen, and in the 9th grade of Junior High, something else complicated my life. A cute boy with curly hair began coming into the diner every evening to get something to take to his job. He was eighteen and working in the cotton mill. One evening Curly asked Mom if he could walk me home. Hardly anyone had a car in those days, and most of the people in Henderson worked, either at the cotton mill or for Roses 5 & 10¢ store downtown.

Before long, Curly, whose real name was Andrew Lee Hunt, asked Mom if he could marry me. But I was still only fifteen, and since I was under-aged, she would have to go to

South Carolina to sign for me. She was so afraid that we girls, being left alone so much of the time, would get pregnant that she agreed. So off we went, with Mom, her boyfriend, Curly's friend, Rose Hughes, and myself. We were married by a lady Justice of the Peace in South Carolina.

Curly and I were very much in love, and so it did not matter to me at the time that he had no money and no home to take me to. We moved in with his mother and father, his grandparents, and his two brothers and four sisters, who all lived together in a big old red house. Boy was I in for a shock! A city girl was finding out what it was like having a big family, and the facilities were far from luxurious.

We had to go across the street to draw water out of a well with a bucket on a chain. There was no indoor plumbing, so we had to use an outhouse. I had never even seen one of those before.

But that was not all. We had to heat water on an old oil stove in the kitchen and pour it into a big tub to take a bath. We drank from a dipper in a water bucket kept in the hall, and we ate at a long wooden table with benches on either side.

There was no doorknob on the bedroom. We would just stuff a sock in the hole. One night, as Curly and I were taking a bath in that old tub, we heard someone giggling. It was his two brothers peeping through the hole at us.

About that time, Mom decided to go back to Richmond where her family lived, so she and my sister packed up and left me with my new family.

Curly worked in the mill from seven to three every day, so he was home in the evenings. My new in-laws both worked in the same cotton mill from three to eleven P.M., so that left everyone at home under the care of Curly's oldest sister Annie Bell (who was just seventeen at the time).

At first, Curly and I slept in the same room with his two brothers, but after Grandma died, Grandpa went to live with his brother, and at last, Curly and I had a bedroom to ourselves.

The big, red house had a long hall with three rooms on one side and three rooms on the other. After Mr. and Mrs. Hunt had left for work, the neighborhood children would come and run through that hall playing. All of this took a lot of getting used to, as these were radical changes in my life.

Curly's mom made biscuits every day. At our house, we had eaten only loaf bread. Other aspects of the food were strange to me. The fatback, fried potatoes, and molasses, and whatever happened to be in the garden at the moment. One day my mother- in-law told Annie Bell to cook fish for supper, while she was at work. She cooked them, but she didn't know they had to be scaled first.

Annie Bell had a boyfriend named Wesley Hughes, who was in the Army. When he came home next, he asked her to marry him. Mr. and Mrs. Hunt said no, so Wesley and Annie Bell slipped off after her parents went to work and got married anyway.

By the time I was seventeen, I was pregnant with our first child. Mom and my sister came down to visit the week the baby was to be born. For a while it seemed that they might miss the delivery, but the last day before they had to go back home, Dorothy Ann finally decided to make her appearance.

Mom was very upset because we had no screens on the windows. She bought the baby a carriage and netting to keep her safe from insect bites.

While they were in Henderson that week, my sister met Curly's cousin, Calvin Wallace, who was in the Marines. They fell in love, and Mom let her stay to help me with the baby. Soon Calvin and Margaret got married and lived with Calvin's parents.

Mom and Dad were still separated when Dorothy Ann was born, so Dad had not yet seen his first grandchild. When we went to Richmond for a visit, he came down from New York to see us. The moment I placed the baby in his arms, he said he was convicted of his wrongdoing. He repented and asked Mom to take him back. She did (but she never forgave him).

He left the other woman and the child they'd had together, and Mom and Dad then moved together to Florida. Dad bought another restaurant there, and they were again too busy for God.

When our baby girl was about a year old, I told Curly it was time for him to get us our own place. He said he couldn't do it, so I took the baby and left to live with Mom in Richmond. About a week later, Curly and his brother John came to get me and the baby. He said he had rented a three-room apartment on the same street as his family. We set up housekeeping for ourselves there, and we were very happy.

CHAPTER 3

SAVED

IN THE APARTMENT ACROSS from us lived an older couple, George and Gladys Watkins. They attended the Baptist church near us and asked me to go with them. One night I did.

They were having a revival. At seventeen, for the first time in my life, I heard the Gospel. Jesus gave His own life to save us from Hell. That night I believed what Reverend Icard had preached and went down to the altar and received Jesus as my personal Savior. Like a child, I believed in my heart and confessed my sins, even though I did not understand at the time what exactly sin was. From then on, I wanted to learn more about Jesus.

My husband didn't understand me wanting to go to church all the time. He would go out with his friends, and I would go to the services. Sometimes I didn't go to church on Sunday night, and, instead, went with him to see a movie.

Curly didn't drink or smoke, so that was good. His best friend was Mack Hunter, and Mack had a car. The two of them would go out riding together, but Curly was always home soon after I was. I began to pray for him to want to go with me to church. I saw other couples sitting together in church, and I wanted that for us.

Curly was a good, hardworking man, but, like all of us, he needed to be born again if he was to get to Heaven. I continued going to church, and I continued praying for him.

I didn't know much about my Bible. I took it to church with me, but didn't yet realize that I needed to read it every day. I kept praying.

Soon I found that I was pregnant again. Dorothy Ann was eight by this time. I suffered a miscarriage, however, and we were very disappointed.

Curly and his brother built us a two-bedroom house in the country. To make ends meet, I took a job uptown at Roses' Luncheonette, and there I met many people.

One of the strangest of these was a lady named Lizzie Harrell. When Lizzie came into the luncheonette, no one wanted to wait on her because she smelled so bad. People sitting around her would get up and leave. I was the only one willing to wait on her.

One day Lizzie came in and kept scratching her head. She took off her hat and said her cat had given birth to kittens in it the night before. She was an eccentric old woman who kept lots of dogs and cats. When she eventually died, she left her money to build a place to take care of her many pets. It was said that she never washed her clothes but, instead, would go to a store and buy new clothes and left her dirty ones there. There are some strange people in this world.

Life was good at the Hunt home. Curly and I were still in love and happy, but then temptation came my way. There was a man who came into the luncheonette every day, and he would flirt with one of the waitresses. Her husband was away in the Army, and she was lonesome. One day she asked me if I would take her to meet the strange man that night. I really didn't think about it being so wrong. I just did it.

That man kept coming in and flirting with her, but I never took her to meet him again. In time, her husband came home, and she quit her job and never saw that other man again.

When Ann was twelve, I became pregnant again, and we had a little boy, whom we named Thomas. We had waited so long for this baby.

Then, wonder of wonders, Curly got saved and baptized. Our little family was together in church at last, and things were good.

Satan could not stand this, and he came to me very unexpectedly. The same man kept coming into the luncheonette, and now he began flirting with me. Just feeling sorry for him at first, I talked to him about the other woman. As it turned out, he was married and had three children of his own and was a Sunday school teacher at another church. He asked me to meet him that night. I was so scared, but, for some reason, I did what he asked.

He only kissed me that night, but that started a lust within me for more, and soon he asked me to run away with him. I really wanted to, and I thought I was really in love with the man. I had married so young, I reasoned, that I had not known what I wanted.

You might ask: how could a married man and a married woman, both born-again Christians, both Sunday school teachers, be so deceived? The truth is that you can sit in church and your body be there, but your mind is somewhere else. It happens.

We never considered how our flirting might hurt other people, but a man who worked with Curly overheard us talking one day and told him about it. Curly confronted me, and I told him that it was true and that I was going to leave him and marry the other man.

How could I have ever thought of leaving my children and my home? All I can say is that the devil blinds people to the truth.

Curly was furious, hurt, and jealous and said that he would put me in a wheelchair and hurt me so badly nobody would ever want me again. This began three years of hell on earth. There was no more happy home for us. Trust had been broken. I had fallen off the pedestal that Curly had put me on. Now I was watched all the time, locked in at night, and not allowed to use the telephone or to see my former friends.

We talked with our pastor about all of this, but he could not believe that I had been serious. I was still going to church and even teaching Sunday school, but in my heart, I was saying, "One day some way I *will* be with this man." I was so miserable, torn between the spirit and the flesh, and I did not know what to do to escape the struggle.

CHAPTER 4

DELIVERED

ONE NIGHT THEY WERE having revival at the Church of God. Ann had been going with Curly's sister and had asked me many times to go too. Being Baptist, I did not go to Pentecostal churches, but when you are desperate and can't find the answer or the power where you are, you go looking elsewhere.

That night, as I looked at the people who were attending the revival, they all looked the same to me — no jewelry, no fancy clothes. I was the one who was different. Suddenly, I wanted what they had. When the altar call was given, I went forward.

I got on my knees and began to cry out to God. He knew the struggle that was going on in me. I wanted to please Him, but somehow I could not get free from the spirit of lust. I just told God very honestly and plainly, "Here is the feeling I have for this man. I can't handle it anymore." I did not know it at that time, but in that moment, I surrendered my will to God.

Oh, happy day! The next thing I knew I was hearing the audible voice of God, speaking to that spirit. He said, "Come out of her." He said it again. The third time He spoke, He said, "Loose her and let go." When He said that, I came up off of that floor like a bolt of lightning and began shouting and speaking in other tongues. God had delivered me.

I don't know how long I danced, shouted, and spoke in other tongues that night, but when I came to myself, I knew I was free and that there was more in God than salvation. All I had known about until then was love and grace and God's saving power. I did not know there was real power for deliverance for every believer.

I went home and told my husband what had happened to me. Because of what I had done, he had backslid and had not been to church since. We began to work on renewing our marriage.

I went back to my Baptist church and told them, as I was teaching the adult Sunday school class, that I had received the Holy Ghost. We had an interim pastor at the time, and his wife was in the class. She stood up and said she did not know what had happened to me but she knew it was real.

I was so full of joy and tried to tell my Baptist friends that the baptism of the Holy Spirit was for anyone who was born again. They said it was all right for me, but they were afraid of what they might do if they received it.

I stayed in that church for six months more, teaching and living the Word. Then one Sunday morning, as I was teaching, the Holy Spirit spoke to me, "Come out from among them. What you are teaching is like water running off of a duck's back."

When I walked out the door that day, I knew I would never be back ... unless it was for special meetings. I had been in that church from the time I was seventeen, and I was now thirty-one, but I had tasted of the deeper things of God, and there was no going back. I had been saved there and water baptized there, and so was my husband. My children were dedicated there. My good friends and my husband's family were all there. Still, it was not difficult for me to obey God and go elsewhere. I knew He had spoken to me.

I was hungry and I had to have more. In the six months since being filled with the Holy Spirit, I had not spoken in tongues again even once, but I knew that I was delivered from that spirit of lust. No one could make me doubt that I could walk past the man and have no feelings of passion whatsoever for him. I was free.

The first time I went back to the Pentecostal church, the Holy Spirit came on me, and I began to speak in unknown tongues again. Praise God, this was real!

Even though Curly had built us a home of our own, life was not easy. He still didn't trust me, and it would take years before I could regain that trust. Believe me when I say that I was ashamed to write this part of the story, but I did it so that someone else could escape the deceptive hands of the devil and God would be glorified in their lives too.

I soon became pregnant again, and Curly and I were blessed with another beautiful little girl. We named her Linda Louise after my mother. She came into my life like a ray of sunshine.

We were living next to Curly's parents, and when his dad died, we decided to move to Boynton Beach, Florida, where my parents lived, and we took his mother with us. It proved to be a new start for all of us.

CHAPTER 5

FILLED

CURLY GOT A JOB WITH the local electric company, and I want to work for Dad in his barbecue restaurant, but not all was to my liking. Dad sold beer in the restaurant, and I refused to serve it to the customers. I had read what the Bible had to say about it: *"Woe unto him that giveth his neighbour drink"* (Habakkuk 2:15), so I stood on my newfound beliefs.

Dad was also open on Sundays, and I simply would not work on that day. He thought I had lost my mind, but I knew I had found Jesus and did not want to do anything to displease Him.

We moved in with Mom and Dad, but they were still too busy working to take time to serve God, even though He had blessed them so much. I started looking for a good church where we could find fellowship. We tried the big Baptist church in Boynton Beach one day, but the people were not friendly to us. I had brought my baby into the sanctuary, and she began to cry. The woman behind me was very rude and told me to take her out, but she didn't tell me there was a nursery.

Next the children and I tried the big Church of God in Lakeworth, Florida. It was okay, but I still didn't feel it was the right place for us.

I heard there was a Church of God in Del Ray Beach, about ten miles south of us, so one Sunday morning we went to find it, but it was not easy to find. We finally asked a policeman, and he told us the church was located in a house on the next street. We found it, and when we walked in, the people were singing and praising the Lord.

It was nothing more than a screened-in back porch, but it didn't really matter because I knew this was where God wanted us. Curly was still backslidden, but I was filled with hope and joy for our future.

We stayed at that church many years and helped to build a real church building. Most of the people there were poor, but that didn't matter. They had love for one another.

We found an FHA house for sale and bought it.

About this time Dorothy Ann fell in love and married a cute guy named Chuck. At the time she didn't yet know that he was an American Nazi and hated the Jews. Chuck was in the Navy, and so they moved to St. Petersburg, Florida, and we soon had our first grandson, Charles, Jr.

My sister Marge and her family of seven children had moved to a big dairy farm in West Jefferson, North Carolina. One day her son Joey, who was seventeen, and his brother

Marty were coming home on their tractor pulling a hay mower. Joey looked back to see if it was okay, and when he did, he went off the side of the mountain. He was killed instantly, but the big seat protected Marty. Joey was going to graduate that next week. We don't always understand why things happen or why God allows tragedy to come into our lives. From the day of the funeral Marge and Calvin never went back to church.

The next year Calvin's brother came to live with them. One morning, they went to the barn, and found that he had hung himself. Marge called Dad. She could not take it anymore. Curly and Dad drove to the farm, piled all they could in the two cars, and brought Marge and her family back to Boynton Beach. Marge was so heartbroken and had worked so hard on the farm. We were happy to have her with us.

By this time, Dad had bought a motel and a restaurant, and Marge and Calvin and their family lived in the motel until Dad found them a house.

The restaurant, called Papa Joe's Place, was a family affair. Dad cooked and sang to all the customers. Marge and I were waitresses. Mom, better known as Mama Lou, was the cashier. My mother-in-law washed the glasses and cleaned the tables. The two grandsons washed dishes. On Sunday, Curly would come in and clean the floors.

Before long, Calvin and Curly started going to the dog track together. Calvin knew all the dogs' names and wanted one day to raise his own. Curly became obsessed with picking winners. Every time you saw him, he was looking at the racing book. Many times, I would put my Bible on top of that book and pray that he would lose all interest in gambling.

Dad gave us a beautiful piece of land on a canal just around the corner from their house and gave Margie and Calvin a lot there too. I had seen a beautiful model home and prayed that we could build one just like it. We did and even furnished it like the model. God was so good to us.

CHAPTER 6

EARLY MINISTRY

IT WASN'T LONG BEFORE Dorothy Ann discovered that Chuck was a Nazi, and he hated Jews. When he got drunk, he called her a Jew. He started abusing her physically as well, and one night he almost killed her. She called us, and we went and got her and baby Charles and brought them to live with us.

Charles was only about eight months old at the time. Tommy, our son, who was nine by then, loved having little Charles around and said that he was his baby brother. Linda also loved the baby.

Dorothy Ann decided to go to work in the restaurant too. We went to church together and to all the revival meetings around.

Along about that time, someone gave me a book that changed the course of my life. The book was, *The Cross and the Switchblade* by David Wilkerson. In that book, he told about how he had established Teen Challenge to work with teenagers to get them delivered from drugs through the power of the Holy Spirit, and his remarkable success was drawing widespread attention.

It was time for Spring break and lots of teens came to the local beaches in Florida and did things they shouldn't do. I felt a prompting from the Holy Spirit to write to Dave Wilkerson and ask him to send someone to go with us to the beaches to give out books and tracts and invite the teens to a church to see the movie, *The Cross and the Switchblade,* based on the book.

As a result, Teen Challenge sent a young married couple and a teenaged boy. All three of them had themselves been delivered from drugs through God's power, and so they had wonderful testimonies to share. They stayed with us two weeks, and what a time we had on the beach each day and at different churches in the area at night. I was happy.

What I didn't realize was that I was neglecting my husband, and this caused him to spend more time at the dog track. Not good!

Dad was getting older and decided to retire. There was a small restaurant around the corner for sale, I thought that Curly and I might buy it, and operate it ourselves I asked the Lord if we should do this, and He plainly said, "No," but I wanted to show Dad that I could do what he had done, so we bought it anyway. That was so foolish because it's always a dangerous thing to do your own thing and be disobedient to God.

At first, we only opened from 6 AM until 2 P.M., and we seemed to be doing a booming business. Then we decided to open for dinner too, and that was a big mistake. Now I had no time for family nor Bible study.

Dorothy Ann and I still went to church together on Sundays, but no longer on Wednesday nights. There was just too much to be done. Soon, even though we were doing a great business, it became difficult to pay all the bills. I was forced to pray that we could sell the restaurant. I didn't know what else to do.

Because of my disobedience, God let us sweat it out for a whole year, and things got continually worse ... until we were nearing bankruptcy. The day before we were to declare ourselves bankrupt, we sold the restaurant. I learned a valuable and hard lesson from all of that: when the Holy Spirit says "No," we'd better listen.

Mom had worked so hard all of her life, and now she was suffering terribly from rheumatoid arthritis. Dad suffered a ruptured appendix, and it turned into gangrene, and we nearly lost him. He had to have a colostomy.

After that, Margie took care of him most of the time, and I took Mom back and forth to her doctor's appointments.

Dad loved to fish, so when he was well enough, he would take our son Tommy to the bridge, and they would fish together. One day, Dad leaned over the edge and lost his false teeth out of his shirt pocket in the water. We kidded him a lot about that.

CHAPTER 7

BACK TO HENDERSON

CURLY'S MOTHER MET SOMEONE at the restaurant and got married again. She had married the first time at fourteen and had never had nice things or been courted or taken to nice places, so she deserved that.

But now Curly began to get homesick for his family and wanted to move back to North Carolina. I didn't want to leave my mother ill in Florida, when she needed me the most, and I didn't want to leave my beautiful home. It was our dream house. Still, I had read in the Bible that a wife should go wherever her husband went, so we sold our beautiful home in Florida, packed up all our things, and went back to North Carolina. The only good thing I could see in all of this was that it would get Curly away from the dog track.

Calvin and Margie had moved to north Florida and begun raising Greyhounds. This meant that Mom and Dad would be left alone for the first time in many years, and that made me sad.

When we pulled into Henderson, I felt sick about it. I really did not want to go back to the place where so much heartache had occurred. Even though Curly promised that we could go back to Florida someday, somehow I didn't think we would.

When we first got back to Henderson, we stayed in that little house Curly and his brother had built for us. Then we decided to buy some land in the country and build a new home. Curly, his brother John, and our son Tom worked together to build us a beautiful split-level brick house.

We went back to the church we had attended before leaving town. They had a five-week revival, and I stood up one night and testified, by faith, that my husband had been saved and baptized and had quit the smoking habit he had developed. And when I had finally believed it in my heart, it actually happened.

One night during that revival, Curly agreed to go with me. The preacher that night preached a lot about the terrible habit of smoking and how to be free from it by the power of the Holy Spirit. I thought to myself, "Curly will never come back to church again." But I had underestimated the power of the Holy Spirit to convict. That very night my many years of praying for Curly to come back to God were answered. He soon joined the church and began singing in the choir. Happy days were here again, and I could not stop thanking God. No more dog track!

Curly, John and Tom had done so well with our own house that they now went into business together building houses for other people, and they were very busy. I took a job at Carolina Comforters. We still had Tom and Linda with us. Linda was now in high school, but Curly and I were so busy with our work and our church activities that we didn't see what was happening with our own children — the same mistake my parents had made with my sister and me. It is hard for me to write about some of the things that happened during that period, but I do so to let others know that God will see you through any and every trial.

Tom had his bedroom downstairs next to the recreation room, and Linda had her room upstairs. Linda had a girlfriend who fell in love with Tom. She would come over and spend the night with Linda, and she and Tom got together, and she soon became pregnant.

The girl's mother would not let them get married because they were so young. Then one day Tom and his friend Douglas ran away, and we didn't know where they were for about two months. Finally, Tom called and asked if he could come home. We were so happy. God had again answered prayer.

When Tom arrived, he brought a beautiful young girl named Denise with him, and introduced her to us as his "wife." We didn't think to ask to see their marriage license. Tom was extremely jealous of her. They went to a party one night, and there was some drinking. The next morning, when Denise came upstairs, I noticed immediately that she had been badly beaten. Her face was all swollen, and her back was bruised.

I began asking questions and learned that they were not really married at all. A group of young people had picked Tom and Douglas up when they were hitchhiking and that's how they had met. I told Denise to go home as quickly as she could.

I didn't know at the time that her mother was an alcoholic and very abusive. Denise didn't want to go home, so she stayed in town, and she and Tommy got back together. We would not allow them to live together in our house without being married. Before long, he beat her again, and she left and went back to Colorado.

Things went from bad to worse. I went down to clean Tom's room one day and discovered that he was growing marijuana in his closet. He had gotten in with a group of boys and girls who were all doing drugs and also started taking drugs. He had a motorcycle and he would come home so high that he would walk into a wall. Only our prayers kept him from being killed.

Even though we had raised our children in church, we had never done prayer and Bible reading in the home. We left that all up to the church. But it is in the home that children must learn to love and respect the Lord and His Word.

One day Tom, along with four other young people in ski masks, robbed a local drug store in broad daylight. Before that, he had gone to Colorado and married Denise, and she was pregnant. After robbing the drug store, he ran away to Florida to keep from getting caught. Denise stayed with us and began to go to church with us.

Denise was like me; she had never heard the story of Jesus, His birth, and His dying on the cross for our sins. She soon believed and accepted Jesus into her heart.

Tom came back from Florida, turned himself in, and was sentenced to eight years in prison. What a heartbreak that was for all of us!

Curly took this especially hard. He had never been in trouble with the law himself and could not accept the fact that his son had done something to bring shame on the family. He refused to talk about the matter or to visit Tom while he was in prison.

Some of the group that robbed the drug store never went to prison.

One day Dad came to visit. He asked Curly why, if Jesus had forgiven *him*, he could not forgive his son. It worked. The very next visiting time, Dad and Curly went together to see Tom. That was another prayer answered. Praise God!

LOSING MY PARENTS

ONE DAY DAD CALLED and said that Mom was very bad off. He had spent much time and money taking her to doctor after doctor, and she had taken every kind of treatment available.

He tried to keep his own personal life going. He would get up, give Mom breakfast, and then go fishing on the bridge and have coffee with his buddies. But Mom's condition weighed heavily upon him.

Finally, thinking that he was doing her a favor, he took her off of all the medication she had been taking for years. She soon went into shock and was in so much pain you couldn't even touch her bed.

When Dad called that day, we immediately got in our car and went to get her. She lay in the backseat, and I sat on a stool beside her, praying and holding her hand on the way back to North Carolina. We took her straight to the famous Duke University Hospital in Durham, and the doctors there began working on her right away.

Mom's knees were bent upward, and she couldn't straighten them out. They put her in traction with sandbags. She remained delusional for the first several days. Finally, she began to improve, but the doctors said she would probably never walk again. They did all they could for her there in the hospital, then transferred her to a rehabilitation facility, to try to teach her how to feed herself again, and they gave her various types of physical therapy.

Our church was praying, and Mom, who was little but spunky, said, "I'll show those doctors! I will walk again!"

I decided to go on a twenty-one day fast for her healing. Every day I would drive to Durham to feed her and encourage her. Every sign I passed along the way seemed to be advertising food.

Dad went back to Florida to sell the house and the business and all of their beautiful belongings, and we brought Mom to our home. She was still in pain and in a wheelchair, and then a walker. Then, one day she just turned loose and started walking from bed to bed.

I took her back and forth to Duke for treatments, but she was soon back in the wheelchair, and I had to bathe and feed her. One day she said, "I don't want you to have to do this anymore."

I said, "Mom, didn't you bathe and feed me when I was a baby? It's my turn now."

It was a serious adjustment for all of us. Mom and Dad were not accustomed to living with two teenagers who played loud music and talked on the phone for hours. Dad would fuss and say, "You should do something about that."

Mom was in and out of the hospital for about the next two years. Then, as I was feeding her one morning, I noticed that she could not swallow and could no longer talk. She had suffered a stroke. We called an ambulance and took her to the hospital.

Dad and I stayed with her. She was in and out of consciousness. We were talking about a woman we knew who had started smoking again, and Mom overheard us and said, "I have *not* started back smoking." She was a feisty little woman.

I wanted to stay all night with her, but Dad insisted that I was needed at home, so I went back to the house. At about 3:00 AM that night, we received a phone call from the doctor saying that Mom had passed away. I could not comprehend it and told him that we would be right there. When we arrived at the hospital, Mom had the most beautiful smile on her face and looked so peaceful. I was sad that she was gone, but I knew that she was with Jesus and would no longer suffer.

Dad was so lost without her. He would get up and go to the mall to talk to other retired men who gathered. Then he would come home for a little while. But he was so restless that he would go back to the mall again. There was one good part to all of this: Dad started going to church with us and was gloriously saved and filled with God's Holy Spirit.

About six months went by. Our pastor's mother, who had been a widow for ten years, was also attending the church. Dad soon swept her off her feet, married her, and they moved to Florida and made each other happy for many years to come. She was a wonderful woman of God and took good care of Dad.

Then one day she called to say that Dad was in Intensive Care and asked if I could please come. It was wintertime, and we had snow and ice everywhere. I couldn't get a flight out, so I got in the car and began driving, praying all the while for God not to let Dad die until I got there.

Margie went too, and we got to spend two days with Dad. He was so happy to see us. He looked at us and said, "I have my three girls with me, and I'm happy." He died that night.

CHAPTER 8

HUNGRY FOR MORE

DOROTHY ANN HAD REMARRIED, and she and her husband Bill were back in Henderson. They now had three children, Charles, by her first husband, and Jeff and Leandra together. One day our pastor, who loved Israel, announced that a lady named Ruth Heflin would be speaking about Israel in a local house meeting. Dorothy Ann and I wanted to hear that, so we went. As it turned out, God changed Ruth Heflin's mind, and she spoke that night about what God was doing in China. We were thrilled anyway.

We had been thinking about going to a campmeeting in Wymama, Florida, but didn't have enough money. We had also considered going to the Church of God campmeeting in Charlotte, North Carolina, but they had no place for children. God had a different plan. As Ruth Heflin finished her talk, she said that they were having campmeeting at Calvary Pentecostal Camp in Ashland, Virginia. That was only a hundred and twenty miles from us. There was no charge for rooms and meals, and there were four services every day. They also had children's campmeeting. Ann and I looked at each other, and we knew this was where God wanted us to go.

When something is of God, He always makes a way. Ann's husband had won some money for selling the most bread on his route that month. He gave her fifty dollars, and Curly gave me fifty dollars. So we had the place to go and the money to get there.

We were so dedicated to our church that we didn't leave for Ashland until after the Sunday night service. By the time we arrived at camp in Ashland, it was already 10:00 P.M., but we were in for a shock. They were meeting in a large outdoor tabernacle, and the meeting was still in progress. Someone was playing a harmonica and someone else was playing the drums, and those who were still there were singing:

I saw the Lord seated on His throne.
He was high and lifted up
And His train filled the temple.

The people had joined together in a long train and were marching around and around the perimeter of the tabernacle, singing and shouting praises to God. Ann and I looked at each other. Even though we were Pentecostal, we had never seen or heard anything like this. She said, "Mom, what have we gotten ourselves into?"

This went on until midnight. After that, the camp office reopened, and we were assigned our rooms. As it happened, they were right above the tabernacle, and some people stayed down there praying and prophesying. Some remained there all night on their faces before the Lord praying. Someone came by and just covered them up with a sheet, as if it was nothing unusual.

The next morning we went to the dining room for breakfast and discovered that there were people there from all over the world. Some were sharing their reasons for coming.

We went to morning prayer, and then attended a class taught by a brother named Jack Chappell.

After that, there was the 11:00 A.M. service, and it was conducted by Mother Edith Heflin, the founder of the camp. She ministered on the Second Coming of Jesus. After preaching each day she would pray and prophesy over anyone who wanted to be prayed for.

The dinner bell rang at 1:00 P.M., but very few people went to eat. They were all very hungry for more of God, and I felt the same way.

When my turn came for Mother Heflin to pray for me, she began to speak in tongues and tell me, "Open up your spirit, open up your spirit, to hear what God wants you to know." My soul was crying out to God, and I could not stop it. I sounded like a woman in labor.

Everything Mother Heflin said to me that day made it seem that she was reading my heart. She told me wonderful things that God was going to do through me and for me, and then she said, "Now dance." I had never felt so much joy before, and I danced and danced and spoke in other tongues. I was not hungry at all for food, just more of God. Later, I lay on the floor and prayed for Dorothy Ann. She was not able to eat the whole week we were there.

After the night service, people would go to the snack bar to eat and fellowship with those who were from other places and countries. I bought Dorothy Ann a hamburger that first night because she had not eaten a thing since breakfast. She took one bite and could not eat any more of it. God was doing something special in her.

The next morning, at the 11:00 A.M. service, they invited everyone to come down to the front and dance before the Lord. The music played, and people began to dance, and it was easy to see that they were having a wonderful time. But I just sat back and watched. I had never seen anything like this before. We had dancing in the Spirit in our church, but each person did it as they were led. Was it right for everyone to get up and dance together in this way? I wasn't sure.

Then, all of a sudden, I said, "Lord, I am going down there and dance, and if this is wrong, please let me know." After only a few minutes of dancing and praising God, I received my first open vision and heard God speak to me. He said, "Daughter, all the kings of the earth have their dancing girls, and when they please the king, he gives them their heart's desire."

He then handed me a large circle with three keys on it, and said, "These are the keys to the Kingdom." I reached out and took them and, when I did, I came back to myself. I had been caught up in the Spirit, and it was wonderful. I have been dancing for Him ever since that day.

The next morning Mother Heflin again asked if anyone wanted prayer. She was a teacher, but also a prophetess of God, who often gave people encouraging words from God or even explicit direction for their lives. This was so wonderful for me. Even though I was born again and filled with God's Holy Spirit and going to church every time the doors were open, church had somehow become a routine. There was no more excitement in it for me.

That morning God heard and saw the hunger in my soul, and she began to prophesy over me again. She said that God had many souls He wanted me to reach and He would work miracles through me. There was much more to her message that God had revealed to her through His Spirit, but that word and that week changed my whole life.

From that time on, I began to feel God's Spirit leading me, and I went home determined to find out what God wanted me to do. I just had to know.

CHAPTER 10

MORE REVELATIONS ABOUT MYSELF

I WAS NOW SUPERVISOR OF the bedspread department at Carolina Comforters, but when I went back to work that next week, I told my boss, a man named Darnell, that I was giving my two-week notice. I had to get back to that camp and find out what God wanted with my life.

I had not yet shared this with my husband.

Darnell asked me what I was going to do.

I said, "Preach the Gospel."

He just laughed. But later that day, he came back and told me he knew that I was serious, and I did not have to work another week unless I really wanted to.

When I told Curly what I had done, he thought I had gone crazy. We had just built another new house, had a new truck and car, and everything in the house was new as well. But, to me, it was a house, but not a home. Both of us were born again and going to church and singing in the choir, but we were very unhappy. We argued all the way to church and all the way back home. There seemed to be a spirit of contention separating us. All of the material things in the world could not satisfy. I simply had to have more of God's direction.

Curly didn't know what had come over me. We had a lot of bills to pay, so it didn't seem like the best time to be leaving a good-paying job. He was still in construction, but sometimes he had work, and sometimes he didn't. He depended on my salary to help us make ends meet. At my work, I had health and life insurance, so when I quit that was gone too. Even when both of us were working, sometimes I had to borrow money from my friend, Eileen, to pay the light bill. God was trying to teach us that He will provide if we will trust Him.

After I left my job, we never had to borrow again to meet our obligations. Curly's jobs increased, and he was able to take care of whatever was needed.

The morning I left to go back to Calvary Camp I had no idea how long I would be gone. The campmeeting began on the last Friday of June and would end on Labor Day in September. Would I stay that long? I didn't know for sure.

Curly was dead set against this, but I just knew in my heart that I had to go. Following the Lord costs giving up our will for His. He became very angry, and, as I went out the door that day, said to me, "If you go, you do not have a home or a husband to come back to." I had to make a serious choice that day: would I obey man or God? I took my seven-year-old granddaughter with me, and off we went.

We stopped along the way and bought a lot of cantaloupes to take to the camp. I was not sad or worried, just anxious to hear what else God had for me. Campmeeting was still in full swing, and I knew that in such an atmosphere of prayer and praise and worship, it would be easy to hear from God. And I wasn't disappointed.

One day they announced that a lady evangelist was coming to preach that afternoon in the 3:00 P.M. service. She did not arrive until 2:30, and she did not know anything about anyone else there (unless the Holy Spirit revealed it to her), and yet she began to call people out and tell them something of their past and then tell them what God had done for them and what God had for their future. She said she saw someone there who was in a factory and there were large rolls of quilted material. I knew immediately that she was talking about me. She said, "You have quit your job, and if you will come down here ... ." Before she could say more, I got up and ran down to where she was.

She said, "You have come out to come in to what God has for you." She told me that God was going to give me "the black heathen" for a treasure and many other things. I knew I had made the right choice and thought I would be going to Africa. It was not until many years later, as I was preaching in our church, that I looked up and saw many black people in the congregation. God spoke to my spirit in that moment and said, "Here are your heathen treasures that I promised." God will always keep His promises to us, even though we don't always keep our promises to Him.

Many people from our church went to camp that year, and God touched them, and they went back with a new life, a new fire, and the church experienced revival. Even Curly came with a group of men, and God filled him with the Holy Ghost. He had been trying so hard and so long to receive, but just didn't know how. When he yielded himself, the Holy Spirit came and took over.

One afternoon, in the midst of all this glory, Brother Chappell and his wife, Pattie, were teaching on inner healing. He was praying for people and asked if he could pray for me. As he prayed for me, he told me there were hurts so deep in me that I didn't even know they were there. Words that had been spoken over me had wounded my spirit. As I went down on the floor under the power of the Spirit, I began to cry and cry and cry. I don't know how long this lasted, but there were other people around me doing the same thing.

After a while, Brother Chappell said, "Now laugh!" I didn't feel like laughing, but he kept saying it. Then he said, "Haw, haw, haw," and as he said it, I began to laugh too, and I laughed and laughed. By the time I had finally stopped laughing, all the hurts were gone. Praise God, I felt so good.

I ran upstairs to my bedroom and began to write to Curly to tell him that I forgave him for all the things he had said through the years that had hurt me. He hadn't even realized what his words were doing.

Forgiveness brings healing. The next day I felt so good. I went back in Brother Chappell's class, and he got me again. He said, "Your children have hurt you and brought shame on your family, even though they were raised in church." Again I was on the floor reliving all the hurt and shame, and weeping and crying out to God. Then laughter came, and I realized that I had been more concerned about my feelings than about what the children were going through at the time, like Tom during his time in prison.

Every day brought new revelation about myself. I realized that I had become self-righteous and judgmental and was full of pride. Mrs. Pentecostal had to fall off her pedestal and repent and be broken before the Lord could use me.

One day, near the end of camp, a short man from India was preaching. He said that he was going to have an International Pentecostal meeting in Eclipse Park in Washington, D.C. As he spoke, the Spirit of God leaped up in my inner most parts and let me know that I needed to be there for this meeting. The next day, as he said it again, the Holy Spirit leaped in my belly. Then I thought, "Oh, my husband would never let me go. I've already been gone for ten weeks." God was testing me again to see if I would be obedient.

It was nearing time to go home, but I didn't want to leave. Then my daughter called and said, "Mom, you need to come home. Daddy is eating and sleeping at Grandma's house, and there is a girl at the restaurant where he eats lunch who is getting too friendly." I asked one of the other women at camp what she thought, and she said I should go home.

I called Curly and asked if he would let me come home. He said he didn't care. I said I wanted to.

I had used all the gas in my car, and I had no money left, so he agreed to put some money in the bank account so that I could get gas for the trip home. Even though I did not want to go home, God let me know that I had been leaving my husband open for the devil to tempt him.

When I arrived home, Curly was watching the news, and he did not speak to me or acknowledge that I was there. Several hours passed, and I began telling him all that the Lord was doing in my life. He should be happy. He had a brand new wife, one whom God was busy changing. He didn't know what to make of it all.

CHAPTER 11

THE NEXT STEP

THE NEXT SUNDAY, WHEN I went to church, just as I sat down in my seat, the Holy Spirit spoke to my heart and said, "You won't be here long."

I laughed and said, "Where am I going?"

I believed what He was saying and said to my assistant Sunday school teacher, Edith, that I would not be there long. She said I'd better shut up because I'd already been gone for the past ten weeks.

I had now been in that same church for twenty-three years, sitting on the same pew, singing in the choir, going to the prison for ministry, teaching, selling donuts and hot dogs to finance the church projects. But I had changed so much that I somehow didn't fit in anymore. I couldn't bring myself to sell another chicken plate or hot dog.

As the day came near to go to Washington, I told Curly about the meeting there and that I wanted to go. I suggested that I might take our truck with a camper on it so that I could avoid motel costs. He said I couldn't take the truck with the camper because he and some friends were going fishing and needed it.

My daughter Ann and my friend Cora wanted to go with me, but none of us had money for the trip or a vehicle to get us there. I asked my brother-in-law if we could borrow his truck and camper, and God must have moved on his heart because he said yes.

We still had no money, but we were determined to go by faith. The next day my daughter called to say that her husband had received some money for selling the most bread that month again, and he had given her twenty dollars. Then a girlfriend called and said she wanted to take me out to eat. As we talked that day, she felt impressed to give me twenty dollars. Then Sister Cora called and said she had been praying about having no money, and the Lord told her to use the money in her billfold. It was money she had set aside to pay bills, but He assured her that He would provide for them when the time came. So, off we went to Eclipse Park in Washington, D.C., as happy as we could be. We had no idea what God was about to do.

Our brother from India (whose name was Samuel) and his partner, Jim, were expecting someone to bring a tent and a sound system and chairs. They were also expecting people from all over the world to be there. When we arrived, there were only about twelve people, plus Brother Wallace Heflin and his staff from the camp. It was drizzling rain. We stood in a circle and began to pray.

After praying, Brother Heflin said he saw how discouraged our brother from India was (even though he had been walking around the camp like a little bantam rooster, so sure he had the mind of God). So Brother Heflin said he would go back to camp and bring a sound system, wood to build a platform, and chairs for people to sit in.

After he and his team had left, I invited our brother and his helper to come to the camper and have some hot soup and coffee. As we bowed our heads to pray, Brother Samuel began to weep. We began to pray for him and prophesied that things would be okay. We then realized that a prophesy given us at camp several weeks before by Sister Viola Weidemann was now being fulfilled. She had told us that we were going to minister encouragement to two men of God, and we would actually feed them. God is so good!

When we awoke early the next morning, Brother Heflin had arrived, and he and his men were busy building the platform and putting together the sound system. To our great surprise, people began coming from everywhere. They were holding up signs. It turned out to be a large union gathering. A demonstration was to take place later that day.

Brother Samuel now had a sign of his own, and he was marching too. His sign said: EVERLASTING REDEEMER ALIVE. This sparked a lot of interest, and we began distributing tracts to the people around us.

We still did not know what God had planned. The union demonstration had been scheduled for 12:00 P.M., but it was delayed until 2:00. When everything was ready, we knelt around the platform and began to pray.

Some bystanders booed and made fun of us, and others sat down in our chairs, some of them eating and drinking. We told them politely that they were welcome to sit in the chairs but that, because we were about to conduct a church meeting, they wouldn't be able to eat and drink there. God gave us boldness.

The music began, followed by testimonies, and then the preaching. We had a captive audience, because the union people had to stay in formation for their march. The wind was blowing softly, and the music could be heard all the way up to the Washington Monument, which was crowded with visitors. If the people had brought the tent, as promised, only a few people could have been reached that day, but God allowed us to be in the right place at the right time, and He received the glory. Multitudes heard.

What a privilege it was to be part of God's plan. We were learning to listen to the prompting of the Holy Spirit and go where He said to go. We stayed on two more days, and people came, and we were blessed, and they were too.

The last evening we were there, we were cooking our supper and our propane gas ran out. I had seen a beautiful motor home parked next to our camper, so I asked the people in it if we could finish cooking on their stove. They invited us in, and that's how God brought about another divine appointment for us.

They were Correy and Jenny Joubert. He was from South Africa, and she was from Australia. They had twin boys and an adopted Vietnamese girl. They also had two other daughters who were studying at Christ for the Nations in Dallas. As the food cooked, we shared why we were there and what God was doing in our lives.

I shared with them that I wanted to start a work for young people who were on drugs. They told us how they had sold everything in South Africa and come to the United States to go to school in Oklahoma to prepare to preach the Gospel. Jenny had been a nurse and Correy a dietician in the same hospital in South Africa. They shared how, when they had finished school, God told them to go to the East Coast because it was very dry there. They had been traveling up and down the coast witnessing, and then God had told them to go to Washington and wait.

We thanked the Jouberts and said goodbye, thinking we would never see them again, but God had other plans. We went home and testified about how God had blessed so many people through our obedience.

CHAPTER 12

A NEW MINISTRY

SEVERAL WEEKS LATER I got a call from Correy Joubert asking me if I still wanted to start a ministry for youth in Henderson. Of course my answer was yes. He said they felt led to come and help us and asked if they might be able to park their motor home in our yard until they found a permanent place. I asked Curly, and he said it was fine. They arrived, and we all prayed about the next step?

Correy asked if he could hold some services in our home. We invited a few people, and they came. As it turned out, Correy and Jenny were wonderful teachers, and in time, more people came.

One snowy morning, a black lady named Delilah came. She used to be my spiritual daughter. God touched her and changed her life. Her marriage was in a mess. She and her husband had three children together, but he had been unfaithful to her many times.

God gave her boldness and she kept coming to the meetings. Her husband thought she had lost her mind and was talking about having her committed to a mental hospital. The evil spirits in him could not stand the God in her.

Before long, our house was overrun with people, and we asked our pastor at the Church of God if Correy could come and hold some meetings there. Pastor agreed, and people came, and the church was blessed.

Many people were so hung up on denomination and so afraid of attending a Pentecostal church that Correy felt led to have some services at a Holiday Inn. This caused a spirit of jealousy to come in, and the pastor thought we were trying to take his members. We weren't. We only knew that if the meeting was held on neutral ground, others would come.

We prayed and asked God what we should do about our vision for young people. There was a big hotel in the middle of town that had been empty for five years, and many home-less people had been sleeping there. There had once been a Western Union office in that building too. Correy and I went to look at it. We prayed and asked God if this was the place He had for us. Then, we found out who owned the building and went to see him.

We had no money and no collateral, only favor with God. The man agreed to sell the building to us for a certain amount of money each month. That had to be God. The old hotel had a hundred rooms and a beautiful dining room. It was across the street from what used to be the train station. It was February when we began cleaning it up, and so cold that we had to work in coats, hats, and gloves.

One of the first things we had to do was shovel out the layers of old newspapers mixed with human waste. We were so happy we didn't care. We sang as we worked to get the place ready to move into.

We realized that this would also be a perfect place to start a new church, but was that really what we wanted to do? We were moving by faith, and I needed to make some serious decisions. Should I leave the church I had been part of the past twenty-three years or should I stay? As I pondered this decision, I remembered what God had said to me when I came home from camp: that I would not be at that church long.

That had happened in September, and it was now February, and I knew I had to go. Everyone in the church thought that I was crazy and had backslidden. Fortunately, Curly really liked Brother and Sister Joubert, and since he was a carpenter, he helped get the hotel in shape. He didn't want to leave our old church, but he would come to services with us on Thursday nights.

We named the church Light House Christian Fellowship, and it was the first integrated church in town — blacks and whites worshiping together. If we went out to eat together or walked downtown together, people gave us bad looks. But we didn't care, because we knew God was no respecter of persons and that He loves and created all races.

One of Brother and Sister Joubert's daughters led the singing, and we sang wonderful songs about the Word and about Jesus. We also began spontaneous singing in the Spirit, as we worshipped God. The other daughter, Virginia, came home too from Christ for the Nations and started a regular school, grades one through six.

As we got each room ready, we began taking in people who needed a place to stay. These were people who were hurting and broken, some of them just out of prison. Because of the new residents and the many other people who felt led to work with us, we conducted chapel service at 9:00 A.M. each morning, then a short break, and then Bible School from 10:00 until 12:00 noon five days a week.

Our teachers were those whom God sent, along with Brother and Sister Joubert. God sent two sisters and a brother, Brother Bill, to live in the facility and help us. We were like one big happy family.

In the afternoons we would all work on the building, scraping walls and painting. There were days when we had no food. Then God would touch the heart of someone who didn't know our situation, and they would bring enough food for us all. We soon had thirty people whom we were training to be faithful disciples of Jesus.

Curly helped too. He went out and bought fifty pounds of potatoes, and we ate what God provided, and He never failed us. (I didn't know there were so many ways to cook potatoes.)

We ate our meals in the big dining room, all laughing and happy. Some of our team learned how to make cassette tapes and mail them out. Some did other needed tasks. Our church began to grow, and there were soon about seventy people in our fellowship. None of our staff people received any money, except at Christmas, when we each received fifty dollars. It continued to be a walk of faith.

VANCE COUNTY

MARK DOLEJS / Dispatch Staff

Dorothy Hunt is the founder and executive director of Life Line Outreach on Raleigh Road. The shelter for women and children is not set up to properly house domestic violence victims. However, they're facing the challenge after receiving an influx of victims during Domestic Violence Awareness Month.

Finding Life Lines

Non-profit organization getting overwhelmed from other cities

> "They've all tried everything before they come here."
>
> —Janice Sticek,
> assistant to the executive director at Life Line Outreach

BY ALLIE RAE MAUSER
DISPATCH STAFF

During the month of October efforts to aggrandize the issue of domestic violence have brought an influx of victims to Life Line Outreach, a shelter in Henderson.

The non-profit organization is set up to house women and children that have fallen victim to substance abuse, suffered financial loss or have mental health problems.

The shelter is not set up to house domestic violence victims, but with calls coming in from overflowing domestic violence shelters, the Vance County Sheriff's Office, and the N.C. Coalition Against Domestic Violence hotline, options are few.

"They've all tried everything before they come here," said Janice Sticek, assistant to the

SEE LIFE/PAGE A8

Let's get down in the trenches with Dorothy

I'm ashamed to say that I do not go to church in the trenches. I feel to be true to my professed religion, that this is precisely what I should be doing.

Dorothy Hunt, on the other hand, lives in the trenches.

I have known of Dorothy's mission, LifeLine, for quite a few years now. When I first heard of her work with the homeless and downtrodden in our community, I expected to run into a person who in my mind had to be big in stature and strong as a mule. After all, to handle all the elements she deals with, all the problems, and all the people that many of us would shun talking to much less invite into our house, she had to be a giant.

Those of you who know Dorothy realize that just the opposite is true. She is petite, tiny even, but brother, believe you me, she's got the heart of 10 lions.

And she can talk to you, also. Conversing with people comes very easy to Dorothy, whether she's known you 10 years or 10 minutes. I think this is one of the many gifts the Lord has bestowed upon her. I suspect her love for all people is her greatest gift.

It seems now that Dorothy has undertaken another seemingly enormous project. She and her organization are ambitiously renovating a structure on Raleigh Road with the intentions of housing 14 additional homeless persons. She has asked the community for assistance in the form of building materials, money, or time in order to complete her appointed task.

Yes, *her* appointed task. She was appointed to this job by the

Fortunately, that's just not Dorothy's style.

Some of the churches in the area do attempt to help Dorothy to a degree. And other churches have programs similar to Dorothy's. First Baptist Church, in fact, was the initiator and a major push behind Jubilee House, which provides housing for displaced families. Several chuches joined with First Baptist in the initial stages of this project to get it accomplished.

Jubilee House is a fine example of the community coming together to give of itself to provide for those less fortunate. A local family donated the property which became Jubilee House. Local churches, businesses, and individuals threw in together contributing time, money, manpower, and materials.

In this case, a structure which was run down and seemingly in need of being razed was brought back to a useful life through the efforts of a unified community.

Now, it seems the time has come for the community to do this again. Dorothy needs us. We need Dorothy too. She is providing a service to our area which those in local government would be the first to tell you would be hard to get funded from county coffers.

And it's helping a segment of

WHIT SUTTON

DAILY DISPATCH
COLUMNIST

remember Mother Teresa. She was the spiritual leader of The Missionaries of Charity.

When she died in 1997 at the age of 87, she left behind a life-long legacy of help and hope for the unwanted, the unloved, the broken, the starving, and the hopeless of the world. She had the unique ability of easily walking into the lowliest mud hut in India or the finest walnut-paneled boardroom in corporate America. Her appeal was universal in scope and unconditional in its love.

Mother Teresa was also a tiny woman who seemed as frail as the white cotton sari which hung loosely about her withered body. And yet, few corporate or religious leaders have experienced the power and prestige this frail woman of God embodied. She did much for the unloved of the world.

We are fortunate to have our own Mother Teresa right here in Vance County. And the work she does for the down and out of our community is no less monumental to our needy than that which Mother Teresa did for the world's needy.

But even Mother Teresa recognized the necessity of enlisting the help of those who could effect change. She didn't mind asking and we didn't mind giving. Now is the time for those of us who can, to donate part of that which God has blessed us with to those who are without.

It's time for the community to support Dorothy, any way we can. As an earlier article pointed out, anyone interested in volunteering or donating time, money, or materials should call Dorothy Hunt

Calvary Campground in Ashland, Virginia

Artists Rendering of Lighthouse Christian Fellowship, 1982

Our First Clothes Closet for the Homeless

Warehouse Donated by Americal Corporation

Safe Haven

Officials of Americal Corp. turn over ownership of a commercial building they owned on Raleigh Road to Lifeline Ministries for its use in providing shelter for abused and endangered women. Left to right: Bob Hubbard, Americal president; Bob Froeber Jr., chairman of the board, Americal; Dorothy Hunt, pastor and director of Lifeline; and Tem Blackburn of the Lifeline board of directors.

The Linda House Donated by Americal

Our Second House Shelter

The Three-Bedroom House God Provided for Me

The Second Church Building: The Lord's Victorious Church

The Trice-Welcome House Donated by Timber Line, Inc.

CHAPTER 13

LOSING MY HUSBAND

AS THE WORK GREW, my husband became increasingly jealous of the time I spent ministering to the people, and this became a point of contention between us. One night we had a special service attended by men from the local Alcohol Recovery Center. Many of them were born again that night, and Curly prayed with them around the altar. After the service, we all went to the kitchen for coffee and cake and were laughing and rejoicing.

I suddenly remembered that I had forgotten to count the offering and put it away, but I also saw that Curly had left and gone home, and, knowing how jealous he was, I decided I should go home too. When I arrived there, it seemed as though he was another man. He asked who I had put to bed and began accusing me of being unfaithful to him. It was as if a knife had turned in my heart. I tried to tell him I had come right home, but he wouldn't listen. He went to bed very angry.

The next morning we were drinking coffee together, and I asked him if he had to work that day. I thought we might spend some time together. He told me he had to go collect some money from a job. I could see that he was still angry.

I had to conduct chapel that morning at the ministry, but I kissed him on the cheek, walked to the door, and then came back and kissed him again. He said, "Why did you do that?"

I wasn't sure. I did need to get to the chapel, but I also didn't want anything to happen to my marriage. On the way to town in the car, I cried out to God, asking Him how long I must be pulled apart trying to please my husband and fulfill my calling at the same time. I was soon to have my answer.

We finished our Bible study and went into the kitchen to eat lunch. Curly came by, and I asked him if he wanted to eat lunch with us. He said no. One of the ladies said, "Brother Hunt, would you get us a big Christmas tree for the foyer? He said he would.

When I got home, I saw his van in the yard, with the back door open, and a can of paint spilled there. I went into the house and cooked him a big steak, with baked potatoes, and onion rings. I would try my best to make up with him.

Six o'clock came, and Curly still was not home. He was always home watching the six o'clock news. It was prayer meeting night, and I had to be back at the ministry by 7:00 P.M. I left him a note to call me when he came home.

I began to worry. I called our daughter Linda to see if he might be at her house. He wasn't. I called his brother John, and he said he had seen him at lunch time. It was raining and cold outside, and I began to think all kinds of things.

Maybe he had gone to check the swimming pool and fallen in. I called Pastor Joubert, and he and about ten men and women came to help me look for Curly.

I called the police, thinking maybe someone had robbed my husband (because the van was open and the paint spilled). The Rescue Squad came to aid in the search.

Our neighbor said she had seen Curly going into the woods with his dog about 4:30. We believed he had gone to chop down the Christmas trees. Everyone kept searching until one o'clock in the morning. Then my daughter Linda went home to her husband and baby. Tom's wife Denise had been going to stay with me, but she went home too.

I finally went to bed, and I prayed, "God, I don't know where he, is but You do, and I trust You. I slept … until the phone rang the next morning at 8:00 A.M. It was the Rescue Squad calling to see if Curly had come home. When they knew he had not, they joined Pastor Joubert and his wife Jenny, some other men and our daughter Linda, searching more of the woods where he had last been seen.

We had a big picture window, and I was looking out of it when I saw Curly's dog come out of the woods. Soon the Sheriff came and told me they had found his body. He had cut down about six Christmas trees, put his hatchet in his back pocket, and then suffered a massive heart attack and fallen face down. They took him to the hospital morgue and asked me and Linda to come and identify him.

As I looked at Curly's lifeless body that day, I heard the Holy Spirit say, "He is with Me."

The next few days were a blur. Dorothy Ann and her family came from Kentucky for the funeral. It was a cold, snowy day.

When you pray, you never know how God will answer. In the sorrow of my personal loss, I now knew that I was free to do what God wanted me to do. A page had turned in my life.

CHAPTER 14

GOD IS MY SUPPLIER

WITH ALL OF OUR DIFFERENCES, Curly had been a faithful provider for our family through the years. Now he was gone, and I was to be tested in a new way.

It is amazing how God knows our every need. I had an old Toyota, and the insurance on it was due. I prayed and told no one about it. The day before the payment was due, a young man I had worked with and witnessed to came by and said he felt impressed of the Holy Spirit to bring me some money. It was just enough for the car insurance. God is so faithful, saying over and over, that He will meet our needs when we do His will.

One of the young women in the church brought a lawyer friend with her to the service. He was so stiff and proper and did not know how to act when he saw us begin to dance before the Lord. But he came back, and each time he came, he loosened up a little more. God's presence was so real and we were learning the will of God.

I really needed a new car, so I wrote Dad in Florida and asked him if I could have my inheritance early, since my husband had passed away, and I was too young still to draw Social Security.

In the meantime, I had an invitation to Morris Cerullo's School of Ministry in Miami, Florida. I would need $100, and, by faith that I would be able to go, I took that much out of an envelope someone had given me and put it with my application. I didn't know how, but I was going!

Dad wrote back to say that he could not send me the money I needed. But, then, about a week later, he wrote again to say that the Lord would not let him sleep until he sent the money. His envelope contained a check for $10,000.

I had intended to buy a new car with that money, but there were so many people in the ministry who needed something that I bought an older car instead. A mother named Del and her daughter needed new shoes. The pastor's wife was going on a trip, and her daughter Virginia needed supplies for school. After taking care of those things, I still had enough money left over to fly to Miami and go to my first school of ministry, plus spend a week with Dad and my step-mother. God still answers prayer.

In a very short space of time, He had shown me very clearly that I had nothing to worry about. Curly had been a faithful husband and provider, but God would now be both Husband and Provider for me.

I decided to give up my house and everything in it in an exchange for the balance of the mortgage on the hotel.

I took a bedroom on the second floor and a small office. After all, I spent all of my time there anyway.

Later I was given a small apartment in the back of the hotel. The only thing I had taken from the house was the washer and dryer, and I now put them in my apartment. Then, one day the man with whom I had traded the house for the hotel came back and insisted that I return the washer and dryer. It was the last thing I owned, except for my car, and, for some reason, it was so hard to let them go. I took them back, but I cried as I did it. I still had a lot to learn about God's goodness.

CHAPTER 15

FACING THREATS

BECAUSE WE HAD SO many rooms, we began renting some of those on the second floor, but we soon discovered that some of our renters were drinking in their rooms, and they were also creating problems. One night there was a drunken man in the hallway talking loudly and disturbing the people in the service. I went out in the hall and told him to go to his room. When he didn't seem to pay any attention to me, I took him by the arm, and, in Jesus' name, escorted him back to his room. He went as meek and quiet as could be, and we didn't hear any more from him that night.

When I got back from Florida, I had another encounter with a young man who was on drugs. We had taken him and his wife in, and they were in a room down the hall from me. Pastor Joubert and his wife lived on the same floor, but had gone away for a few days. The only other person on the floor at the time was the janitor.

I had just finished studying a lesson from Morris Cerullo's material about standing toe to toe with the devil and not backing down, when someone knocked on my door.

I had on my pajamas and robe and was ready for bed, and when I opened the door slightly, the man pushed his way into my room. He proceeded to sit down on my bed, and began to growl at me like an animal. He then ripped open his tee shirt. Before I knew what I was doing I grabbed his arms and commanded the devil to come out of him in Jesus' name. He went limp and just looked at me and said, "You really are a woman of God." I took him by the arm and led him back to his room. How thankful I was that I had studied that lesson and that no fear had come upon me, only a holy boldness.

Thank God for the men and women who have fought the battles and won the victories, and then passed on to us the knowledge of what they have learned.

The spirit of fear is one that will always try to stop us, but God's Word teaches us that we can overcome through Jesus, who is in us. To accomplish it, we must face each ungodly spirit and use God's Word to overcome it. This was what Jesus did as a man in the wilderness. He knew Gods Word and used it to overcome. I was to learn a lot of valuable lessons in the next three years.

We took in another man and his wife. She was pregnant and had not felt the baby move, so she was very upset. We prayed, and then I took her to Duke Hospital to have an ultrasound done. The doctor allowed me to go in with her as the test was being conducted. We could see the baby on the screen and the doctor was pointing out the various organs, when the baby suddenly put her hand up and waved to us. What a joy it was to know to see and know that the baby was indeed alive!

That mother was so thankful that the next Sunday she repented of her sins and asked Jesus into her heart. Her husband did not get born again, and we eventually had to ask them to leave, which was sad. I had grown to really care about them and had done all I could do for them.

Here's what happened: One evening a group of us were standing outside the hotel talking, and she asked to borrow my car. I said no, and she turned on me and was coming at me to hit me. Thank God some of the staff members grabbed her and then ordered them off the property. I was so hurt and disappointed, after all we had done for them, that I went upstairs and threw myself on the bed and cried and cried. I swore, "I will never help anyone again."

That lasted for about two hours. I got myself together and went down to the prayer room, and we all prayed for them. It was about two months later when she came walking down the hall toward me. It was dark and long, and no one was in sight. A sudden spirit of fear came on me. I just knew she was going to hurt me.

As she came nearer to me, she was saying, "Please forgive me. I don't know what came over me." And she began hugging and kissing me. She had come to see if I would go with her to the place they were staying to pray for her husband.

I found one of our sisters, Sister Del, and asked if she would go with me. She said she couldn't. I found her brother Bill and asked if he could go, and he said he also couldn't. Against my better judgment, I got in my car to go to the house, which was just a few blocks away. I was very frightened that this was some kind of plan to harm me.

As fear was attempting to overcome me, I remembered what the Bible said: *"For God hath not given us the spirit of fear; but of power, and of love, and of a sound mind"* (2 Timothy 1:7). I knew then that God was with me. (If I had not gone, I would not have overcome that fear.)

As it turned out, her husband was very friendly and, after a little while, I asked him if he wanted to accept Jesus in his heart. He said yes, but when I told him he needed to forgive anyone who had hurt him, he said, "I can't forgive the man who shot my brother, who died in my arms." I told him that God would help him forgive that man and that if he refused to forgive him, God would not forgive him. But he just couldn't do it.

I left that day feeling very sad but knowing I had done all I could. Being in the ministry and having to deal with all kinds of people is never easy. You have to face all sorts of hindering forces.

CHAPTER 16

LOSING ALL

FOR THE NEXT THREE years we were in that hotel everything went well. God was saving, delivering and filling, and people were being transformed. Things were going so well that we were preparing to open a satellite Bible school. I was to be the Dean of Women, and Rev. David Dunlop had agreed to be the Dean of Men. A large satellite dish, donated by a couple in our church, had already been installed and ready for operation. Applications for the school were coming in, and classes were to begin in September.

Correy had brought his mother over from South Africa. She was a precious lady. Then his brother also came over, and that's when things began to change. Correy's brother was rich, but he was not born again. In fact, he was an alcoholic and soon began playing cards with some of the residents.

I saw a change come over Jenny and Correy too. They decided to have an interior decorator come in and redo the rooms, and they wanted to rent the rooms to the elderly. They also wanted to open a restaurant in the foyer. They got in the bad habit of opening the mail, taking out any checks that had come in to the ministry, and not even reading the enclosed letters. Some of those letters were from students enrolling for the fall classes.

We had placed large ads in a magazine, and they needed to be paid. I began to feel very upset in my spirit and told Brother and Sister Joubert that I needed to go away for a few days to fast and pray. During that time, God gave me scripture that let me know I could no longer respect our current leadership.

They had made a contract with the Employment Security Commission (ESC) to house thirty immigrant workers. They were to feed them breakfast, a bag lunch, and dinner. That was not what God had called us to do. I went to Brother and Sister Joubert and let them know I could no longer be a part of the ministry, since our purpose for starting the ministry had changed. They, in turn, told me that I was no longer welcome, even in the church.

The following Sunday they announced publicly that anyone who had anything to do with me would be disfellowshipped. This was my hometown, and these people were my friends. I had not moved out yet, and afterward many of the members came back to my apartment to ask me what was wrong. We'd had about seventy regular members, but the next Sunday there were only some thirty.

The Jouberts and I talked and, since the hotel was divided into two parts, they agreed to take the front (the newer part), and I agreed to take the back (the older part).

When I went to my lawyer to draw up the contract, he advised me not to do this. To be in the same building with those who harbored hard feelings would not work. I still wanted to start a teen challenge for young people, and I thought now might be a good time to do that, but I took the advice of my lawyer and did not sign the contract.

The next Sunday there was only the Joubert family and two other people left in the church. How ugly, Christians against other Christians. I am sure the devil was sitting back having a heyday. What had started out good had now ended up hurting many people and all because of greed.

What should I do now? My daughter Dorothy Ann and her husband had become missionaries to Sitka, a small island in the southern part of Alaska, and they now sent me a ticket to come and visit them. I was so hurt, with no home and nowhere to go, that I thought I would die spiritually.

I agreed to go for a twenty-one day visit, but every time I started to go home, the Lord would say, "Not yet." I was okay with that. Alaska was so beautiful, and the church they attended there had such loving people in it that my hurts began to heal. I was enjoying my grandchildren and the beauty of the lush green mountains and the beautiful ocean.

I went to help one of Dorothy Ann's friends pack to move. As we were packing, she picked up a book and told me that she felt the Lord wanted her to give it to me. It was *Basic Youth Concepts* by Bill Gothard. Later as I looked through the book, I came to a page about the eight callings of God and I could see I was in the 6th step, the fire. Fire, he said, either destroys or purifies. I was being tested by what was going on in my life. In the fire we are refined and learn endurance. This helped me to see what was happening to me.

Another page in the book said that your vision has to die so that God can supernaturally bring it back to life. It related how many Bible characters, such as Moses and Joseph, had to go through the death of their vision. It was easier to go through it when I understood what God was doing in my life.

I went to spend some time with another woman of God, and she, too, gave me a book to read. It was the classic *In His Steps* by Charles Sheldon. I was able to share my hurt with her, and she told me to forgive, and God would take care of the rest. I was unaware of what was going on at home, as I had no contact with anyone.

After a stay of two whole months, I arrived home to find the hotel padlocked and some windows broken out. That wonderful new satellite dish had been ripped out, leaving a large hole in the roof. Most of the furniture had been sold. This was all so difficult to face.

God sent my dear friend, Yvonne, to me from Massachusetts, and together we went in and knelt down amid the broken glass and prayed. I did not know what had happened.

I went to the city council to ask why the doors were padlocked. They told me that the Jouberts had put the migrant workers on the third floor to sleep, and the third floor was unfinished and was not to be occupied until it was inspected. They had given the Jouberts forty-eight hours to move the workers. Instead of moving some of the other renters, they had put the migrant workers in the basement, and that, too, was unfinished. So the city had gone in and condemned the place and then padlocked it.

The Jouberts had sold most of the furniture and left town with the proceeds. I looked at the mess and broke down and cried. Now what was I to do? No home to go to, and the rumor had been spread around town that I was involved in the occult.

I thought of going back to Alaska or to Florida (where my son Tommy lived), but after I prayed, God told me to stay put and let those who had misjudged me see what He would do. It would have been easy to run from a bad situation, and to stay and face the problem was not nearly as easy.

CHAPTER 17

STARTING OVER

I HAD LEARNED HOW to make cassette tapes, so now I went on a local radio station on Sunday mornings and also bought a tape duplicator and began sending out copies of the messages. One way or another, I would continue serving the Lord.

I have always had a heart for the poor and broken. It seemed as if there was always some young woman in trouble and needing a place to stay. My two Christian sisters, Brenda and Delilah, had this same desire, so we prayed together and decided to take women into our own homes (I had begun living in Dorothy Ann's mobile home). The three of us would meet several times a week and pray. Soon we each had two people in our home to minister to.

It didn't take long to find out that this was not a good thing to do. These people had serious problems. We began looking for a building to house and train these women, to enable them to find a new way of living.

One day I was taking one of the women out to clean someone's house, and I decided to go down a road I had never been on before. I passed a long cement-block building with a FOR RENT sign on it. It had a steeple on it, like a church, I thought to myself, "We're not looking for a church," but I backed my car up anyway and wrote the phone number down.

This happened on a Friday. I still had hope in my heart that God would let me go back to the hotel and start over. That Saturday night my daughter-in-law came over and was very upset. She said, "Mama, the hotel is on fire. It's burning down. Come and see." But I could not bear to go and see my dreams and life's savings go up in smoke.

The next morning, as I was on my way to church, I had to pass by the hotel. All that was left was a shell of a building, and there was smoke still coming out of the windows. My heart was broken again.

After church, I went home and lay on the floor asking God why He had let this happen. I kept blaming Him and crying. The phone rang, and it was Brother James, one of our members. He told me that God had spoken to him to come over and pray for me. I was glad to have someone to share my sorrow with. I had been so determined to go back to that hotel, but God had allowed it to burn to the ground because I wanted to have my way. I didn't yet understand that God had another plan.

Just before James arrived, I said, "God, what am I going to do now?"

I heard Him say, "Call the number in your pocketbook."

Brother James came, and I told him what God had said. We called and arranged to meet the owner of the building the next day. Brenda, Delilah, James, his wife Dorothy, and I all went to see it.

We entered to find a church sanctuary with gray walls, gray pews, an old, faded carpet and a rickety Bible stand. In the kitchen were a broken refrigerator and a lot of cobwebs, nothing more.

There was also an office and three Sunday school rooms. The owner, Mr. Edwards, told us he would rent it to us for $300 a month. We formed a circle and prayed, but before we prayed we decided that if we all came to an agreement, we would take it. After prayer, we all felt God had led us to this building, so we took a giant step of faith and paid the first month's rent. We had exactly $300 between us.

I had long ago quit my job to go into full time ministry. Brenda had no job, and Delilah was raising three children alone. Only James and his wife Dorothy had jobs. We did not know how we would pay both the rent and the light bill. We were poor, according to some people, but we knew were rich in faith.

People began bringing beds, sheets, towels, soap, and even a stove and refrigerator. We turned Sunday school rooms into bedrooms. Brenda and I moved the women in and began having daily devotions and prayer. We didn't advertise our needs, but God moved on people's hearts to bring just what we needed, when we needed it.

On Sundays, we would take our little group of blacks, whites, and one Mexican girl to different churches in the area. People stared at us — a white woman holding a black baby. They didn't make us feel very welcome. The churches were still all black or all white, as if God hadn't Himself formed all races. Thank God a few churches were beginning to rid themselves of prejudice.

We started having our own services at the building. I knew God had called me to be a pastor, and now I stepped into that role. One day, during prayer, on the floor on my face, God had impressed me: "I have called you to be an under-shepherd."

I said, "Lord, I don't even know what 'an under-shepherd' is."

That next Sunday morning my pastor preached on The Under-shepherd. Jesus, he said, was the great Shepherd, but He had many shepherds under him.

At a conference with Norvel Hayes in Gatlinburg, Tennessee, God spoke to me at the altar and said, "I have called you to be a pastor." It was the second time he had told me this.

I said, "How can I be? I don't have the education."

Why is it we make so many excuses when we know something is from God?

The third time he called me I said, "Yes, Lord, if You show me how, I will obey." I have found that if we will only obey His calling, He will equip us for what He has called us for. Little did I realize that He had already been preparing me.

We named our new church "The Lord's Victorious Army."

God sent an evangelist by the name of Leah Gilbert. I had met her in Florida. We also had gone to Calvary Camp the same week. When they introduced people from different places, I stood up and said who I was and where I was from, and then Evangelist Leah stood up, and we were surprised to meet each other again.

After the service that day, Sister Leah told me she was led to stop in Henderson and come to the church. She'd had a vision of the church building and described it to me perfectly. I was glad to be in the right place at the right time.

When Sister Leah arrived in Henderson, she had her nine-year-old son with her, and they stayed to work in the ministry. Now we were both responsible for children, and neither of us had any income, just a burning desire to serve our God. He had done so much for us that we were determined to serve Him by serving the poor and needy. According to Matthew 25:34-46, this was our calling. By doing it *"unto one of the least of these,"* Jesus said, you have done it *"unto Me"* (Verses 40 and 45).

The ministry began to grow ... until we had no more room to put people. One day a lady called us and said she had a mother and two children whose husband wanted to kill her. Would we take them in? I said we had no room. Where would I put them? Then I reconsidered and told her to bring them anyway. We would put them on sleeping bags in the office.

When the lady came, I told her I was ready to quit if the Lord did not give us more room. She told me of a big house in the country that she had looked at and said she would take me there the next day to see it. It was in a place called Middleburg.

It was a beautiful two-story farmhouse about seven miles out of town. We found out who owned it and how much the rent was. It was $300.00. A doctor in town knew of our situation and the need for more room. He said if I would take it, he would pay $100 on it each month. It was another step of faith, and God was stretching us and teaching us to trust Him.

BUILDING A SOLID FOUNDATION

NOW WE HAD A church and a ministry to house and care for twenty women and children. I still had no paying job or other income and was too young to collect Social Security. We prayed for everything as we needed it.

One day I told the people we had a light bill due the next day for $67.40. We all gathered in the living room to pray. There was a knock on the door. It was a man who had brought a young girl in trouble to us three weeks before. When he asked to see her, I told him she had left two days before. Before he left he put some money in my hand and thanked us for helping her. The amount he gave us was $70. Our God had come through again. He has promised us that He is the God of more than enough, but He usually tests our faith until the last hour. God was still working, and He had a plan bigger than we could imagine.

The next week a lady from Vocation Rehabilitation called and asked if we would take a young man who was still in prison. He had been eligible for parole many times, but his family was in New Orleans, and he was required to have a home plan and a job before he could be released. He was in for cashing a federal check when he was seventeen and had been in prison for ten years already. He was now twenty-seven. I don't know why I said yes, but I did.

The woman made arrangements to bring the young man to us in a few days. His name was Larry, and he had no idea that he was coming to live in a church with an old lady. When he arrived, he was surprised, but he was so glad to be out of prison that it didn't matter to him.

I learned that Larry was Italian and had been a cook in the prison and had men working under him. Larry became my spiritual son and still is today. He would go into the sanctuary and sit, and God would give him songs that he would then sing in the church.

We began to take men in and Larry looked after them. I would bring the girls in on Sunday morning and evening and on Wednesday night to be with us in church. We were like one big happy family.

Then Leah's spiritual son and daughter came from Florida to help us. Melvin became the assistant pastor and his wife Ginger taught the children. Sister Delilah and her husband Richard were our song leaders.

Soon we met a man and his wife who needed some counseling. Melvin and I went to their house and prayed with them, and they gave their hearts to Jesus. Sam was a truck driver and had lived a rough life. He had scars on his neck and face where he had been cut. He should have served many years in prison, but, by the grace of God, the judge had set him free. After Sam's salvation experience, he found a new way of living. He hadn't known there was any other way to live except fighting and trouble ... until he met Jesus. Sam's wife Andrea loved the Lord and would laugh and laugh and laugh and get down in the Spirit.

Sam and Melvin got the young people together and began to train them to be in God's Army. They had to earn their fatigues by doing community service for some older people, cutting grass or doing whatever else they needed. We had an old green van, and Sam would go to the projects and pick these young people up. They had seen and known too much for their age. They really needed a male figure in their lives, because most of them had never had a father in the home. They began to know what it was to serve God by serving others.

One night during a revival the evangelist prayed for Larry, and he went out in the Spirit. When he came to, he was saying, "No, not her!" He was leaning on a pew looking dazed. When we asked him about it, he said the Lord had told him to marry Kathy, and he was saying no.

Kathy was one of the young leaders in the shelter. She had a beautiful little girl named Bettney who was three years old. Guess what? Within about two months, Larry and Kathy were married. It was the first wedding in the church. God met our every need and still does.

I must tell you about a young black fellow who came to a revival meeting. His name was Waverly, and he was very religious and quiet. One night the evangelist laid hands on Waverly, and he received the baptism of the Holy Ghost. He was shouting and jumping around and speaking in tongues.

He had been going to get married and then, two weeks before the wedding, his fiancé had died. When he first came to us, he cried a lot. In time, those wounds were healed, and he also became one of my spiritual sons.

After he received the baptism, I changed his name to Timothy. He was no more Waverly. He is now married and has two children and is a pastor in his own right. God can take a shy and broken person and change them completely. I write about these people because I know what God's love, grace, and power can do.

We took in an older man named Alvin. He had a bad problem with alcohol. Before he came to us, he had been sleeping in an abandoned warehouse. One night some boys beat him up and stole his leather jacket and all his money. After we had taken him, one day we went to town to buy groceries and left him alone at the ministry. When we came home, he was drunk, lying in the flower bed in front of the church.

We should have dismissed Alvin then, but, instead, we gave him another chance. He gave his heart and life to Jesus and was delivered from alcoholism. In time, he found a woman, and they got married. You could see them walking together in town, holding hands. They both had dyed their hair red, and he had on some funny-looking plaid pants that he always wore. They looked so funny, but love has a way of covering our faults.

One day a man came to our house in Middleburg and asked to speak with me. He said his name was Rhem Hutchinson, and he was the Executive Director of the Alcohol Recovery Center in Henderson. He said he had been watching my life for a few years and that I was where he had been twelve years before. He gave us our first real offering — $300. He also said that he wanted to introduce me to some people from the United Way because they could help us. He arranged the meeting.

Because we did not yet have our 501 (c) 3 status, we did not qualify for help from the United Way, so we filed our papers for tax exemption. We did not yet have a board, so we didn't qualify for that status. We formed Life Line Outreach, Inc. with a duly qualified board and applied again, and this time we were approved. The United Way then gave us a grant of $5,000. God had provided for us in yet another way.

When the board members learned that I had received no salary since starting the ministry, they approached their churches and raised $400 a month for that purpose. I had never done the work for the money, only for the love God had placed in my heart for people, but I appreciated their generosity nevertheless. God rewards us for faithfulness. It was good to be able to buy myself some much needed things. Our God knows all our needs, even before we ask Him.

I must share about one of my spiritual daughters. Her name is Martha, and she, too, had a problem with alcohol. Martha and her daughter Felicia, who was eight years old, and Martha's mother Sally had been living with Martha's sister Jean. Jean and her husband Arthur had bought a double-wide mobile home and had to rent a small apartment while the house was being set up. They did not have any room for Martha and her family, so someone sent her to the shelter.

When they arrived at the shelter, Martha had been drinking, and she refused to stay the night. Sally and Felicia stayed. The next evening Martha came back, because she had nowhere else to go but the street.

We were all getting ready to go to church, and I told Martha she had to go with us. She protested, because she had been drinking again that day. She was wearing a red bandana on her head. That night there was a woman preacher who gave her testimony of how God had saved her and delivered her from alcohol. Martha went forward to receive Jesus as her Savior, and He not only forgave her of her sins but also delivered her from alcohol. That was eighteen years ago, and Martha has never taken another drink.

Today Martha has her own apartment and Felicia's grown and has two children of her own. Martha is very dear to me, and I have been her spiritual mother ever since. God can do great things in our lives, if we will only believe. I could go on and on telling of the miracles He has performed.

One of the thrills of helping these young women is being able to be with them and see firsthand the birth of their babies. I didn't think I could watch, but it was such a miracle to see. What a joy to see the expression on their faces when they first see the baby and find out if it's a boy or a girl.

Most of those babies have no visible fathers, and it is very hard for a single woman to try to raise a child alone. (Some of them have several children.) Instead of looking to God to help them, most of them are looking for men. Thank God some of them stop having illegitimate children.

My heart goes out to the children. They have been in so many homes — grandmas, uncles, aunts, and friends — until people get tired of them and put them out. Once we accept them, it takes about two weeks for them to realize they are safe and loved.

CHAPTER 19

NEEDED EXPANSION

ONE DAY ONE OF our board members came and asked if we would like to go and see a two-story brick house in town that was for sale. Of course, I said Yes, but we don't have any money to buy it. Several of us went with them.

The house was so nice. It had central heat and air-conditioning. We really needed to get closer to town, as the house in Middleburg was seven miles out, and we had to make the trip several times a day — for someone to go to Social Services, a doctor's appointment, work, or the Welfare Office. Within two weeks God had made a way for us to get this house. It was wonderful not to have to make that long trip so many times and not to have to make a fire in the wood stove on cold mornings.

Before we moved into that house, a lady called and said she had a lot of clothes she wanted to give us. Could I meet her at the church? It was raining and thundering and lightning, but I decided to go anyway. Just as I started out the back door, one of the ladies said, "You had better come get this umbrella." At that very instant, lightning hit a huge oak tree nearby, and it fell right through the door I had been about to go out. God saved my life that day. He is an awesome God.

When I sing the song about how awesome He is, I then ask Him, "God, what are You going to do next?" He just keeps on blessing and blessing, as we obey His will.

A hosiery factory called Americal owned a large warehouse, a three-bedroom house, and an empty building that once had been a factory. The warehouse butted up against our backyard. One day I asked one of the board members if he would ask someone at Americal if we could rent the long building to open a thrift store to train the ladies how to meet the public and run a cash register. We also needed to find some additional income to keep the ministry going.

After about a month our board member came back and said, "How would you like to own the whole property?" I could not believe it! Americal had just opened a new distribution center and needed a tax write-off. It was another great miracle for us.

The property is on US 1 North. It now houses offices (where we do our counseling), a church, food storage, and downstairs is the thrift store. The building we wanted for the thrift store is now a homeless shelter for twelve single women. I and the staff live in the three-bedroom house. We have an extra bedroom that can accommodate two ladies, when we are full at the shelter, or we can take in someone who needs extra attention.

To get the ministry started I had sold my car, and then, when my husband died, I had traded our house for the rights to the hotel. God had assured me He would always provide a place for me. For quite a while, I had been sleeping in one of our shelters with the ladies. Now I had a place of my own where I could to live and rest.

We were still having services where we started, but across the street from our new beautiful brick house was a big white church with a fellowship hall and a big yard. It was for sale. Again the board asked if we would like to have it for our own church. I could not believe it and, again, I said, "But we have no money to buy it." Someone signed a note, and soon we were in that big church. It had Sunday school rooms upstairs and a good sound system. We began to grow faster, as more people came, and God saved and delivered many.

Now God had brought us from a small beginning to more responsibility, and now we needed more room to house the many brokenhearted, unwed mothers and those with addictions. God had told us, in Isaiah 58:3-8, what a true fast was, and promised that if we would set the captives free, He would provide.

A company named Timber Line, a manufacturer of wood products, had just bought a new warehouse in Henderson and in front of it was a huge modular home that had been offices for a mobile home plant. They were getting ready to take it down, to landscape the new place. My niece's husband Tim was their accountant, and one day, when he was in the office, he overheard them talking about bulldozing that house. Tim said, "Why don't you give it to Life Line. They need more space to house women and children?" The owner called and asked if we would like to have it? Another answer to our prayers.

Now we had to find someone to move it, and we would have to get permission from the city to put it on our property. After a lot of reasoning and permits, they said we could do it. First the home had to be cut into four pieces so that it could be moved. Only God knows what it took to get it ready, but it all got done.

Since we had a large mortgage on the brick house, we decided to sell it. We did not put it in the hands of a real estate agent and had no idea how quickly it might sell. We put a sign in the yard, and within a month the house was sold.

We were now in another dilemma. We had no mortgage, and that was great, but the new place was not ready. We had to find a place for all the people from the brick house to live in the meantime.

CHAPTER 20

WHAT GOD WANTED

I ATTENDED A CONFERENCE in Charlotte, North Carolina, where John Kilpatrick and Steve Hill from the Brownsville Revival were speakers, and there I witnessed something I had never seen before and have not seen since. When the altar call was given, people came running to the altar to receive Jesus. All the chairs at the front had to be quickly moved before the altar call began. People ran and even slid on their stomachs to get to God. There was no need for begging or pleading. These people were so hungry for more of God's glory.

After all the people were ministered to, all the pastors were asked to come to the platform for special prayer. As we prayed, every one of us went out in the Spirit, and God began to speak to us about His glory.

The next Sunday, just as I stepped into the pulpit back home to speak, suddenly God gave me a revelation of what He wanted. I asked two men to come and put the podium down to the left side, on the level of the people. Then I told another man to take the big chair where the pastor usually sat and put it where the pulpit had been. Then I got the big family Bible opened to a picture of Jesus and sat it in that chair. All the congregation was wondering what was happening, and there was an awesome hush.

I began telling them what God was showing me and saying to me. He said, "I am tired of man or woman getting the glory that belongs to Me." The Bible represented the Word, which is God, and so all the praise and glory belongs to Him. He was to be the center of all we did. From that day on, the pulpit remained on the left of the platform on the same level with the people. Many people were born again that day because they saw and felt the manifest presence of God. Oh, what an awesome God we serve!

God had a plan, but we could not yet see it. Our mortgage payment on the big church was $900 a month, and this was a lot for a congregation of about a hundred and twenty-five people. Our tithes were dropping. One of our prominent families, a doctor, was transferred to Chapel Hill, and another family was transferred to Florida. This mortgage was now a burden for the people, so we got together to seek God about what to do about it.

God told us to sell the church and pay off the debt. It was a hard decision. We were to take part of the warehouse and remodel it for a church. Just like the house, the church sold in three months, the debt was paid off, and we were debt free.

The Lord's Victorious Church moved into a beautiful sanctuary in the warehouse. A picture of Jesus with His arms outstretched was painted where the pulpit would have normally been. On the side wall was a picture of the children of Israel coming through the Red Sea, with Moses standing on a big rock holding up his rod. We put in chairs so there was plenty of room for dancing, just as Miriam and the women of Israel had danced and played the tambourines.

Now all the property was debt free, the shelters, the thrift store, and the new triple-wide was almost ready to be occupied. We had to have new wiring put in, because when the people moved it, they'd had to cut the wires underneath. We had to put in three regular bathrooms and a handicap bathroom. And, since the new building was designed for housing, we had to put closets in each room.

Many people from the community came and volunteered their time to help. Sears in Henderson donated a beautiful stove and stainless steel refrigerator. Thomas's Appliance donated a large microwave. One of the members of our church donated ceramic tiles for the bathrooms. Warren Furniture Exchange donated a complete bedroom set with a queen-sized bed. The Masonic Home was putting in all new beds and donated bunk beds and mattresses.

Churches began to hear about our need and brought sheets, towels, and washcloths. The plant manager of Pacific Feather (formerly Carolina Comforters), where I used to work, donated pillows, comforters, and dust ruffles. One lady called and brought seven boxes of restaurant dishes. Someone else brought enough silverware for all. Burger King donated fourteen chairs. In this way, the whole place was furnished by the community. It houses a large family room, an entrance foyer, ten bedrooms, and a playroom for the children, complete with toys.

A beautiful mural was painted by Fran Vaughan on the dining room wall. I have found that nothing is impossible with God, if we have faith to ask and believe.

Everything was finished by December 15. The first mother we received, Sonya, a former drug addict who had been in our program for four months, was told that her five children could come and spend Christmas week with her. They came, and it was a joyous time. We put up a tree and decorated the house. People in the community brought presents for all.

Sonya's husband was in prison, and the children had to go back to their grandparents' home. Sonya completed her program. During that time she was born again and delivered from drugs. She later became our house supervisor. Today her husband is drug free, and they both have jobs, and the children are with them. To God be the glory!

CHAPTER 21

THRICE WELCOME

ONE DAY SONYA BROUGHT in her friend Renee and Renee's seventeen-year-old daughter Jeannie, who were both pregnant and both had a drug problem. We took them in, and both mother and daughter gave birth while they were in the shelter. Renee had a beautiful baby boy whom she named Noah. Jeannie had a beautiful blond-haired girl.

Renee's husband, who was also Jeannie's father, was in prison. Both mother and daughter came to our church and were born again. Renee got a job as a dental hygienist, and soon they graduated from our twelve-step program called Celebrate Recovery (a ministry we started in 2003). They rented a house nearby and continued coming to church.

Not too long after that, Jeannie got married, and she and her husband Mike now have another baby girl. Our God can do the impossible, if we let him. Nothing or no one is too hard for Him.

Three years passed, and the house was full of mothers and children. We named the house Thrice Welcome, for the

God the Father, God the Son (Jesus), and the Holy Ghost welcome those in need to share the house they have provided.

It is now 2013 and Life Line Outreach, Inc. is thirty-two years old. Only God knows how many women and children have passed through our doors. We are the only homeless shelter within a fifty mile radius. I am thankful that God called me and gave me a heart of compassion for those in need.

There are many scriptures in the Bible where God talks about helping the poor and brokenhearted. My personal commission has been Isaiah 61:1-3. When I first read these scriptures, I knew what God wanted me to do:

> *The Spirit of the LORD God is upon me; because the LORD hath anointed me to preach good tidings unto the meek; he hath sent me to bind up the brokenhearted, to proclaim liberty to the captives, and the opening of the prison to them that are bound; to proclaim the acceptable year of the LORD, and the day of vengeance of our God; to comfort all that mourn; to appoint unto them that mourn in Zion, to give unto them beauty for ashes, the oil of joy for mourning, the garment of praise for the spirit of heaviness; that they might be called trees of righteousness, the planting of the LORD, that he might be glorified.*

God has sent many women to us to find a new way of living. I wish I could say all of them do, but the truth is that even after hearing the truth, some go back to their old ways.

And God has sent me some wonderful co-workers who have given up their plan for His plan and have given up their life for others. The Bible talks about losing one's life to truly find it. His way brings perfect peace, love, joy, and contentment.

Marta is one such lady, and she has a wonderful testimony. She moved to this area with her two children from Chicago to escape the gangs and killings there and lived here with a relative. She soon discovered that this relative was a Muslim and was trying to convert her. Marta was herself on drugs but really wanting to quit. Someone told her about Life Line, and she came and was delivered.

We went to get her two children, but they were locked in the house by the relative and could not get out. We called the police, and they took the children forcibly out of the house. The relative was very angry and wanted to argue. We just got the children in the car and left. Now, three years later, Marta is our business manager and grant writer and my right hand. What a change God made in her life! And her story is typical of so many. Thank God for all of them. God has performed so many miracles for Life Line, and I pray that we will never get so involved that we fail to recognize them and be thankful for them.

CHAPTER 22

TAKING A SABBATICAL

I HAD BEEN TRYING for three years to win a Sabbatical from the Z. Smith Reynolds Foundation, but each year someone else won. The fourth year, when I received the announcement for the sabbatical, I said that I would not try again. Janice Stricek, my administrative assistant, took it upon herself to fill out the application, then she reworded my story and turned it all in — fifteen minutes before the filing deadline. The result was that I made the top ten and was called to go to Raleigh for an interview. I could take Dorothy Ann, and the foundation would pay all of our expenses. It was very exciting!

The morning of my interview I was the first to tell the committee why I needed a sabbatical and what I would do with it. They gave me thirty minutes to speak, and then they were to question me. I began to talk and tell them what was in my heart, forgetting all about the time limit. When the committee finally stopped me, they said I had answered all the questions they had been prepared to ask and that I would have their decision within a few days. A week later I received a call from a representative who said that I had received a three-to-six-month sabbatical with $25,000 cash, to be spent any way I chose. I also got to name two other organizations that would receive $5,000 each. When this news came, all of us in the office shouted and praised God.

My board gave me permission to go, as long as I made sure all the staff knew what to do in my absence. During those months (I chose four), they would not be allowed to contact me, and I would not be allowed to contact them.

Janice found and reserved a cabin in Butler, Tennessee, for three of those months. My desire was to spend time alone with God, and to rest, fish, and start writing a book about all that He had done in my life until then.

I decided to go on my sabbatical beginning May 1. Before I left town I saw an advertisement for a prophets' conference in Knoxville, Tennessee. I sent in my registration. I did other things. My brother-in-law was in Henderson from California. My niece, Sue, had a beach house at Topsoil Island, and they invited me to go there with them. My other two sister-in-laws were also invited, and they went. What a wonderful way to start a vacation, with family. Because of my work, we had not been able to spend much time together for years.

Sue's house was beautiful and only two blocks from the beach. I would get up early and go for a walk on the beach, then just sit on the sand and watch the waves. I would think about how big God was and pray.

We went shopping, and we went fishing. It was all so relaxing, after being at work eight or nine hours a day for so many years.

Sue, her daughter, her daughter's friend and her husband were flying to Orlando, so I decided to go with them. I had been planning to drive to Florida for my son Tom's fiftieth birthday anyway, so Sue booked me a seat on the same plane with them.

Orlando was still about a hundred and fifty miles from my son's home, so I rented a car and drove there. My sister Margie and lots of nieces and nephews also lived in that area. Tom was raising his two daughters, Nicole and Jessica, there, and I got to spend a whole week with them. Tom took me fishing on his boat, and I caught a five-pound bass. I don't know who was happier, Tom or I.

My sister Margie and I planned a surprise birthday party for him and invited all the relatives. We told Tom to come over to Margie's house for a spaghetti dinner. He was surprised. My heart's desire to spend time with them was being fulfilled. Because of the money from the grant I was able to take the girls shopping and to eat out. I had never been able to do that before.

I had to fly back to Raleigh for some training concerning the sabbatical and stayed at Sue's home in Raleigh overnight. I met our instructor and the other five sabbatical award winners. God was stretching my horizons with new friends and new places. It was a time of forgetting the cares of the ministry and just relaxing and having fun.

We stayed at the Roundtree Hotel. It was luxurious, and I had a beautiful suite, with my bed turned down for me every night and chocolates on my pillow. The two days of training were very enlightening and informative.

After leaving there, I called my daughter, Dorothy Ann, and my grandson, Phillip, and his wife Lisa and their two-year-old son Phillip to meet me in Durham, and we went to the zoo in Asheboro. What a wonderful time we had, taking pictures of all the animals and of each other. We spent the night at a hotel, went swimming in the pool, and ate out. God is so good! These were things I had long wanted to do with the family and never had the time or the money to do them. Just to be with them was wonderful.

They went home to Henderson, and I went on my new adventure. I stopped for two days and nights in Boone, where my nephew's daughter Angie and her family lived. I had such a nice time with them. I even went to church with them. What a beautiful family — mother, father and two children, a boy and a girl! We went to a large park and had a picnic and played ball. These were things I had not taken time to do in a long while — be with family and just have fun.

I went on to Butler to my cabin and stayed for a week before that conference I wanted to attend began. I got lost going to the conference, but eventually I arrived safely and went to the motel just a few miles from the conference site.

The first night of the meetings, we were late getting out, and I hadn't had supper, so I decided to go to a Shoney's to eat something. I didn't know it, but God had a divine appointment waiting for me. As I was going into Shoney's, there was a group of ladies and two children going in together. I asked them if they minded if I sat with them, since I was all alone. I didn't know they had been at the very same conference. They were all from Johnson City, Tennessee.

We talked and fellowshipped until twelve o'clock that night. Three of the ladies and the children then had to go home, but the other lady, Kathy, was camping nearby in her truck. As we talked, Kathy said she wasn't sure she could find her way back to the campground. I said, "Why don't you spend the night at the motel with me. I have two double beds." She agreed.

I soon learned that Kathy was also in ministry. Her work was called Mercy Child, and they did street evangelism to the homeless. We had so much in common that we talked until about three o'clock in the morning about all the good things God was doing in our lives.

We went back to the conference the next morning. The praise and worship was so wonderful that people were dancing and waving flags. I was right up front dancing with them.

One of the staff people came and took me up on the platform, and we danced along together. Suddenly the joy of the Lord hit me, and I began laughing so hard I could no longer stand. I collapsed on the floor laughing, not realizing that I was right in front of the speakers. They prophesied over me. What a service it was!

That evening, the speaker was James Cole. As he shared about what God was doing in his life, he, too, started laughing and fell out, rolling on the floor with laughter. He was still laughing half an hour later, and he was so drunk in the Spirit that some of his staff members had to pick him up and carry him home. He had said earlier that he was going to pray for everyone there before he left. Needless to say, he was not able to pray for anyone that night.

Kathy stayed with me until the end of the conference, and when we were ready to leave, I asked her if I could follow her home, since she lived a town near where my cabin was located. All the way there, I felt as if I was on fire. The air-conditioning was on in my van, but the Holy Spirit was all over me. Then great joy came over me, and I knew God was up to something.

We stopped for me to get some supper (Kathy had been fasting since the night I met her), and as I was eating, she said, "Woman of God, God just gave me a new assignment." I asked what it was, and she said, "I am to look after you and serve you for the next three months." I knew immediately that this was from the Lord. The cabin I had rented was off by itself, with woods all around. I was not afraid, but my family and staff had been concerned for my safety. Having a companion would be wonderful.

Kathy followed me to the cabin, and when we got out, I told her that I had three bedrooms and three bathrooms and that she was welcome to stay with me if she wanted. I was downstairs, but the upstairs rooms were empty. She said she had been asking the Lord for a quiet place where she could put up her tent and spend time with Him. In back of my cabin was a long green strip, the perfect for the tent.

In the days to come, Kathy would not disturb me until she saw me out on the deck. Then she would come over and have coffee with me and tell me about what the Lord was showing her and what she felt He wanted her to do. She had prayed and anointed a building in downtown Johnson City that would be perfect for an office, a coffee shop, a stage for a band and preaching. The building was right in the town square, where she and her coworkers did street ministry on Fridays and Saturdays. She invited me to go see the building with her, and I did. We anointed the door of it and prayed that God would open that door for her ministry. Kathy had already seen a vision in which the door was open, and she was in the building. We were believing for a speedy fulfillment of that vision.

For the next three months we listened to Bible teaching tapes and visited many churches in the area. One day I mentioned to Kathy that I wanted to learn to operate a computer. She went right to her storage locker and brought me her own computer. Then she taught me how to send and receive e-mails on it. Anything I mentioned to Kathy she did it.

The cabin was beautiful and well furnished, but it did not have a recliner. She went to her storage unit and brought me her own recliner to use. We were so compatible, and it was easy to talk with her. I called her "my angel."

We went together to another conference at Shekinah Church. I had been there once before. It was located in a beautiful old barn that had been refurbished. The pastor was Sue Currin. They had a guest speaker from Nairobi, Kenya. The night before we went I had a dream of a big outdoor coliseum, and there were people shouting and dancing in the aisles. The seating appeared to be something like that of a sports stadium.

When the speaker gave his testimony, he told how God had blessed him so much that no church building could now accommodate his congregation. Then he showed us a brochure of his ministry, with a picture on the front, and it was just like I had seen in the dream. Before I had even seen the brochure, God had impressed on me to give them $1,000.

Many other wonderful things happened during my sabbatical. I especially enjoyed my times with family members.

I invited my other son-in-law and his family to come up and spend a week. Charlene, my daughter-in-law, and her six-year-old daughter and my grandson, Dustin, came. We went to the Tootsie Railroad, rode the train, and got shot by the outlaws who boarded it. We saw them fight the Indians and we rode the other rides and had another great day with family.

The next day I rented a pontoon boat for the day, and we went sightseeing on the river. We took turns being pulled on a big yellow inner tube. I fell off trying to get on, but I can swim, so I eventually got on the thing, and then the captain pulled me so slowly I had to tell him to speed up. He tried to throw Dustin off, but couldn't.

We got in kayaks and paddled on down the river, and the captain came and picked us up. Then he took us to a beach, and we swam and played there. By the time he got ready to cook our dinner right there on the boat, we were all hungry. We went back to our cabins exhausted.

Money was not an object this time, and to spend it on loved ones was such a pleasure. What a joy it was to be so loved and so free from the responsibilities of the ministry and having the finances to spend on things I had long wanted to do!

I decided to invite my grandson, Phillip, and his wife, Lisa, and my great-grandson, Little Phil, to come up for a week as well. We all loved to fish, so I rented another pontoon boat, and we went fishing.

The captain of the boat took us to places he knew fish would frequent. Little Phil had a Spiderman fishing pole. We used crickets for bait, and, at first, I was afraid to put them on the hook, but I soon learned. We caught so many fish and had so much fun. It was a beautiful day.

The Captain then took us to a beach where we could go swimming. He took a nap on the boat while we swam. By the time we had finished swimming, we had worked up an appetite, and he cooked hotdogs and hamburgers with all the trimmings right there on the boat. Even as we were returning to the dock, we were still trying to catch more fish. What beautiful pictures and memories!

Later that evening, we sat around and talked, and Lisa made a wonderful spaghetti dinner.

The next day they wanted to go to Dollywood. We arrived there about 1:30, bought our tickets, and began to see the sights. But then a terrible storm came up, and they had to close the park. We were given free tickets to come back the next day. On our way to the van, we all got soaking wet.

We had planned to spend the night nearby, so we had to go to Walmart and buy some more clothes. That night we ate at a big steakhouse. Then we got rooms in a local motel.

We were up the next morning and back to the park for a day of fun. We rode rides and saw shows and took more pictures. We finally arrived back at the cabin, tired and happy. Sadly, they all had to leave so that Phillip could go back to work.

Whenever family came, Kathy would go to her mother's or to Johnson City. When she came back, I went with her again to do the street ministry. I saw firsthand people sleeping in the square and one man washing his feet and socks in the fountain.

Kathy had her daughter-in-law and other ladies helping her. I met her family — her mother and sister and a dear friend named Katherine. One day I decided to take them all to see the famous frescos at two different churches, one in West Jefferson and the other in Jefferson. They were done in hot lime. At the first church we visited that day was a fresco of the Last Supper covering an entire wall. Someone had installed a recording that came on and told about the fresco. It was so awesome that we looked at it three times before leaving.

Then we went on to St. Mary's Church where we saw another fresco that covered the entire wall. This one was of Jesus on the cross. Again a recorded message told the story of the fresco. In the basement of that church were other frescos, of John the Baptist and of Jesus and Mary.

Before finishing the day, we went to a family restaurant named Greenwood. It was another lovely day in which I was able to share my good fortune with others.

All too soon it was time to end my sabbatical and head home, after four wonderful months away from Life Line Outreach. It had been wonderful, but I was ready to resume my responsibilities as Executive Director.

CHAPTER 23

BACK TO WORK

WHEN I ARRIVED HOME, I found that many changes had occurred. One of the ladies who had been with Life Line for eight years had suffered a nervous breakdown and had left her office a mess, with papers strewn everywhere. It took a while to get it all organized again.

Another office worker, who had kept all the official records of the ministry, had left for a better-paying job, and a new lady was filling in for her. She was both smart and efficient, but it didn't take long to learn that she had a drug problem, and I had to dismiss her. Then I had to find the right person for that job.

Marta, the lady from Chicago, had come in as a resident and had worked her way up to house supervisor. I found that she had many talents.

Marta wrote a grant request to the Cannon Foundation for $25,000 to remodel our food pantry and, praise God, we got it. Our old pantry was very small, and we had six old freezers. We were able to hire carpenters and build lots of shelves and divided the USDA pantry from the new community food pantry. We were able to purchase a large walk-in freezer and two roll-around upright coolers.

It took about six months to get everything up and working, but now we were able to give food to the community every Tuesday and Friday. We buy food from the Food Bank for our thirty-two residents and those who come to visit. And we will continue to help people find a new way of living, as long as the Lord provides.

It never ceases to amaze us how He meets our needs. Praise His name! Walmart Distribution calls us when they can't receive trucks, and they send them over to us. One time we received 800 pounds of bacon and 50 cases of hot dogs in this way, not to mention many other things. We call around to other agencies and share with them when we have a surplus, and, of course, share with the needy all over our community.

Our program has grown to be able to teach the ladies computer skills on site. We also have contracted with Vance Granville Community College to get the ladies their GED certificates. And we have developed a Christian version of the twelve-step program for those with addictions. Our business manager, through the Ker-Tar Regional Council of Governments, is able to help the ladies who have disabilities to find housing, with their rent fully paid.

Most of the women (and children) who come to us have been hurt and abused, some physically and some mentally, and they need God's love. He recently brought a young lady into our lives who had been deeply hurt by her family. She gave up her own life and belongings to take care of her mother, who had Lou Gehrig's Disease, and faithfully cared for her for fifteen long years. Then, when her mother died, her brother and sister took everything and left her with nothing, and she suffered a nervous breakdown as a result.

Before all of this, she had served in the military and was in the medical field. We found her at a Bible camp, walking around depressed and lost, looking for someone to love her. She came to Life Line Outreach and lived in the house with my daughter and me. We soon learned that she had many talents. Within two weeks, we found her something to do. She began transporting the ladies to their appointments and became our full-time transporter.

This sister is able to give out medications twice a day to those who need it. She has started going to a local flea market each Saturday and selling items from our thrift store. And she refuses to take any pay for it. She just wants to serve the Lord.

She also cleans and cooks at our home. I am eighty-five now, and my daughter is sixty-eight, so we can't do as much physical work as we used to do.

The woman has a pug dog who lives in the house with us. Tupper is like her child, and we all love her.

We discovered that this woman had never applied for any Veteran benefits, and we helped her do that. At one time, she sold ATM machines and didn't realize she was still earning money each time someone used one of them. We took her by the bank one day, and she was surprised to find that she had money coming she didn't know about.

What a change has come to her life since she came to us. She is happy and loved and has found her place in the Lord's work. God is blessing Life Line Outreach every day with divine favor. He overwhelms me with what and who He sends.

In January of 2012 I was blessed to be able to go to Morris Cerullo's Thirty-Ninth World Conference. There were people there from all over the world. The theme of the conference was NOTHING WANTING FOR GOD'S PEOPLE. WE WOULD FIND DIVINE FAVOR. During that wonderful conference, God allowed me to give offerings to help spread the Gospel of His soon-coming Kingdom, and I did not give to get.

I read a brochure from Brother Cerullo called *God's Victorious Army,* and it made me realize how very much God has blessed me since that trip. When I got back home, there was a letter from the Social Security Administration saying that they owed me $620 and had deposited it into my bank account.

I went to the dentist to have him repair my partial plate and put in two new teeth, and when I went to pay him, he said, "I feel led to donate this work to you for all the work that you do for the poor and homeless." It was $350.

That weekend I started laying hands on those who were sick and praying for them. I did the praying, but God did the healing.

One of my staff members called. She said she saw a woman being attacked by a spirit of fear and oppression. We took authority over those spirits and cast them out and replaced them with peace, love, and joy. What a blessing to be doing what Jesus did!

My daughter and I used to do these things all the time, but in the midst of the work of caring for so many people, we sometimes forgot to just do what Jesus did. We were getting back to basics.

That week a man whom I felt had cheated the ministry out of some money came from another town and said, "I feel that I owe you $100," and he pulled it out of his pocket and gave it to me. Two days later a lady whom we had helped said that she wanted to bless me and also gave me $100. I praise God that this is my year of divine favor, and I am to reap the harvest from many years of sowing.

That night my grandson came by to bring Dorothy Ann's cellphone to her. As I hugged him, God told me that he had a need. The same $100 the lady had given me I gave to him. He was touched by someone caring. An offering is not something you owe; it is something you sow. It was good to be back to work, doing what I do best.

CHAPTER 24

THE CHANGING TIMES

BY 2010, I REALIZED that we were living in very different times and people were somehow different. They were not as thankful for the provisions God had made for them. Jobs were harder to find, and so many of the ladies had to stay longer than the usual six months. One lady, who was middle-aged, went to Vocational Rehabilitation, and they found her a job in Raleigh. She was able to save enough to find her own place, moved, and is very happy and still attending church.

Another lady, Jackie, had been at Life Line for fifteen months and could not find a job. She began taking care of an elderly lady and found a place she could call home.

The years are passing so quickly. In August of 2012 Elizabeth was made manager of our thrift store, and she and a resident made it into a very attractive and organized place to shop. They set sales records. What a blessing it was to see God using people to further His work!

In July of that year, I celebrated my eighty-third birthday, and I again began taking some time off to be with family.

Dustin, my youngest grandson and his wife now had a new baby girl. They named her Linda Riley, after his mother, who had passed away in 1999. They were living in Orlando, Florida, where Dustin was going to Harley Davidson school to be a motorcycle mechanic.

My youngest great-grandson was turning six, and I got to spend a whole weekend with him and his parents. It was wonderful. We went swimming, and played ball (even though I had to sit in a chair to pitch), and Phillip ran after the ball for me. We went fishing, which is still my favorite thing to do, and his, too.

Life Line continues to take in homeless and broken women and children, and we do all that we can to teach them a new way of living, so that they can have hope, love, and understanding, as well as food, shelter, and clothing. What a joy it is to see the difference in their appearance and behavior in just a few short weeks! Many of them come to church with us and are born again and baptized, and begin to grow spiritually. God is still in the business of saving and changing lives. I give Him all the glory.

We, the staff at Life Line, will continue to reach out and reassure people until Jesus comes for us. We will never know how many lives we have touched by this ministry until we get to Heaven. Until then, the story goes on.

It is my desire that whoever reads this book will be inspired by what God can do with an ordinary housewife without a high-school education, but a willing vessel to hear

His call to do what Jesus did. As I continue to follow Isaiah 61:1-3, step by step each day, I fully expect to one day hear Him say, "Well done, my precious daughter." To God be all the praise and the glory.

As I offer to you this final Amen, I am now eighty-six, and God has not finished with me yet. Praise His Holy Name!